Relentless Pursuit

Allecia Marie

Contents

DEDICATION

There are many people who have contributed to my ability to see the pursuit of Jesus in my life. To all of you who played a part in any way with this pursuit, thank you. Through big and small moments, you have shaped my story. I recognize that I would not be sitting here, sharing this story with you all, if it wasn't for the ministry school I attended at Bethel Church and the class of 2020. There, I was marked by the pursuit of God and was able to see where He was in all parts of my life. To the leaders who made space for me to see that reality, thank you. For the class of 2020 who pursued God with reckless abandon, you've changed my life for the better. I am forever indebted to you, and the passion of pursuit you carry from knowing you are relentlessly pursued. From the bottom of my heart, thank you.

Why I'm Writing This:

When I looked back over my life, I was able to see where God was in the moments that I started following Him. But I couldn't see where He was before that, in the middle of brokenness and pain. In the middle of unbelief and doubt. In the middle of rebellion and sin. Was He a God that was just waiting around for me to come to Him, or was there a possibility He was pursuing me the whole time, even when I couldn't see it? And if He had been pursuing me, what did that look like? My hope is that through reading this book, you will see the goodness of God's hand in my story. I pray that you will experience the same relentless pursuit in your own life. I hope you will know He pursues every human being with that same unrelenting love, during the best parts of your life and in the moments when you had no idea where He was. I also pray you would accept the invitation that God is inviting you to, seeing the relentless pursuit of His heart for you. It is by no accident that you are reading this book, as there is an open hand He has outstretched toward you. The Father is pursuing you and always has been.

In the interest of being as authentic as possible, throughout this journey we are about to embark on together, I have chosen to share different aspects of my life through stories, personal experiences, journal entries, poems, etc. By including these and choosing to be transparent with my story, my desire is that you will feel connected to my stories in a more personal way, hopefully resonating with your own life in some way, shape, or form. Next to every chapter's title, I have included a worship song I feel connects to the corresponding chapter's theme. Feel free to listen to these songs as you reflect on what you just read. I know how uplifting these songs have been to me and hope the same for you.

I'm so grateful you're here, and I know this book will be impactful to you! Not because of anything I have done, but because of the One who has changed my life. *Relentless Pursuit* has been saturated in prayer, and every single one of you who will read this has been prayed for as well. God cares for you so much and is on a mission to capture your heart. He loves you, friend, and so do I.

He has extended an invitation to you. What will it be? Will you reach out and grab His hand to go on this journey with Him? Will you let Him show you what pursuit looks like?

Let's go on the journey together....

Relentless Pursuit

RELENTLESS: a synonym for this word is persistent, which means continuing firmly in a course of action in spite of difficulty or opposition.

PURSUIT: to follow someone in order to capture.

PURSUE IS AN ACTION WORD, REQUIRING ACTION TO PURSUE. THIS action has a goal in mind, which is to capture something or someone. Jesus is firmly and persistently on a course of action to capture your heart, which requires movement on His part. Even in the midst of difficulty and opposition, like the definition mentions above, Jesus continually and firmly pursues us. It is by no accident that you are reading this book. He is pursuing you and always has been. Will you let Him show you what pursuing looks like, some of you for the first time and for others, going deeper into what that means from heaven's lens?

You never outgrow needing to be pursued, and Jesus never outgrows wanting to be pursued by you either. Jeremiah 29:13 (NIV) says, "You will seek me and find me when you search for me with all your heart." He has extended an invitation for you to come on this journey with Him. What will you choose?

The journal entry below was written a year before I graduated from college. I was in a place where I was seeking God and desperately wanting Him to meet me in that search. However, I didn't know at that time I was craving to be pursued by a God who intimately knew me and understood me. Little did I know this would begin the journey of seeing His pursuit of me from the very beginning of my life. I was becoming aware of His constant pursuit for me, and it was only the beginning of discovering this truth.

June 15, 2016:

All I've ever wanted in life was for someone to fight for me, to prove that they will never let me go. Letting another human being try to fill that desire though ultimately leads to being unsatisfied and unfulfilled. However, there is one person who has fought for me since day one.

Jesus decided to pursue me from the beginning and solidified that promise the day He laid down His life for me on the cross. Ever since then, He has recklessly pushed past all barriers to get to me, torn down walls to reach me, and used circumstances and people to drastically bring me back to Him, because He knows I'm lost without Him. I've truly realized this past year how even when I thought He had abandoned me the year before, He was in the

*middle of creating a beautiful story in which each piece fit
perfectly into a puzzle to make me whole again.*

Each situation kept bringing me closer to Him until Jesus knew
He had my heart for good this time, and He didn't plan on
letting go. Because that's the thing; He will never stop pursuing
me. A father's love is fierce and knows no limits, and my heavenly Father shows me that daily. That will never change, and it
encompasses who I am as a person. My identity is love because
He first loved me, and His relentless love has won my soul. My
hope is that through reading about the pursuit of the Father
through my story, you will accept the invitation He has
extended to you as well. The invitation that brings you to deeper
freedom, the empowerment He gives to live with purpose, and
the transformational experience of being captivated by the face
of a good and loving Father.

Bring It All To Peace

("Peace": Amanda Cook)

WHEN YOU THINK ABOUT PEACE, WHAT DO YOU THINK ABOUT? Is peace a mindset, a habit we put into practice, or an experience you've tangibly felt before? Is it a lack of anxiety, a feeling of bliss perhaps, or an unwavering in the toughest of situations? Some people think peace is something to obtain; others believe it is a gift to be received. I'd like to suggest that peace is a person, and that person comes close to you in spaces and times where peace doesn't seem to make any sense.

Do you know what it feels like to have someone step into your pain with you? To comfort you in the middle of mourning; not necessarily providing all the answers, but somehow their presence is enough? Their mere existence surrounding you makes you feel less alone, less isolated. There is a humility that can be seen in a person who chooses to step into your circumstance with you, a vulnerability of letting your own heart be exposed in

5

those moments, and a healing that comes from the other person simply meeting you where you are at. Some of the best conversations in the middle of pain don't have many words at all. Rather, there is a lot of listening, crying, empathy, closeness, and a willingness to sit and be there with one another, bringing peace.

Closeness makes us feel seen, heard, valued, and cared for. Closeness gives us peace, hope, and joy. The closeness of God came and met me when I was seven years old, and it forever changed the way I perceived God moving forward.

But I'm getting ahead of myself, which I tend to do. Let's go back to the beginning of where this all started.

I was born and raised in the small state of Connecticut, which is typically known for the popular TV show *Gilmore Girls*, beautiful autumns and arguably some of the best pizza spots in the nation. Summers were spent at the beach; autumns spent pumpkin-picking and finding the best apple cider donuts (my personal favorite!); winters were for hibernating and hoping school was cancelled; and springs were waiting games on whether you would have more snow, or if we would skip right to summer! I come from an Italian family, so homemade sauce and Sunday pasta dinners were a staple in my household, regardless of the season. I have a younger sister that I was (and still slightly, ok more than slightly) obsessed with. (Side note: Before she was born, I would pray for a sister and exclaimed to my mom that if I got a little baby brother instead, I would cook him in the oven and throw him out the window.) Quite a vivid imagination. Thank God Jesus answers prayers! I spent my days getting my sister to follow along in the plays I created for us and being the star of any video camera that came my way.

Life was good from what I knew, but little me couldn't have possibly been prepared for what was about to come. I was six years old when my parents sat me down to let me know they were getting a divorce. I would find out years later the reasons behind this decision and understand completely, but to me, the word "divorce" had no significance. It wasn't a part of my story (yet), so I didn't understand it.

"Do you have any questions, Allecia?" they asked after telling me the news.

Nope, I was only six. If I knew the next steps of this decision meant that we had lost the deli my family owned (where the customers would occasionally tip me if I helped make their food), and my mom, sister and I would be moving in with my grandma, I might have posed a few more questions. But I didn't. So, to Grandma's house we went for the next year. (So much love and respect for that woman!)

If there are two things that are true about me, since I practically came out of the womb, it's that I never stopped talking and I never stopped asking questions, which definitely made for some interesting report card comments throughout the years! My mom vividly remembers a specific time, where I held her face in my little hands and asked her who made her face. I was, and still am, fascinated by the way things work, seeing all sides of every situation and wanting to know why things are the way they are.

My little brain was always thinking and pondering the big questions in life, even from an early age.

In terms of faith, my mom had started bringing us girls to church a few years prior to the divorce because she thought it would be good for us as a family to instill morals and values in my sister and me. I can only imagine the questions that must've gone through my little head sitting in Sunday school classes. I must've been ruminating on some thoughts for quite some time, which led to me finally asking my mom a question I couldn't quite seem to figure out on my own. This specific moment is engrained in my head permanently, as it was a marking moment for me in my faith journey.

I was in the backseat of the car while my mom was driving. I can remember that it was dark out, and I sat staring out the window, looking up at the sky, a question forming on my lips as I thought deeply about something. "Mommy, how do you give your life to Jesus?" I asked. She explained to me that you need to believe that Jesus came to die for your sins and was resurrected to have eternal life with anyone who would simply believe in Him. I needed to admit I was a sinner in need of a Savior and know that I was forgiven by His grace.

Little seven-year-old me continued to stare out the window and then, coming to a decision, declared that I wanted to give my life to Him. We prayed together when we arrived home that night, and I accepted Jesus into my heart. I chose Him in that moment, but what I would go on to later realize is that I only was able to choose Him because He first chose me. There was a lifelong pursuit of God after me that had started way before I was even born. He has always been pursuing my heart, even when I wasn't aware of the reality of that truth yet.

"For He chose us in Him before the creation of the world to be holy and blameless in His sight. In love He predestined us for adoption to sonship through Jesus Christ in accordance with His pleasure and will to the praise of His glorious grace, which He has freely given us in the One He loves" (Ephesians 1:4-5).

A year later, we moved into our new house. My mom decided that she wanted us girls to have a life full of stability and, at the urging of her current boss, had gone back to school to get her degree. She moved us two girls into a home where we would stay all throughout our childhood. My mom is, by far, the strongest woman that I know. We never went without a home-cooked meal, and she always prioritized family by creating moments to bond with her children. She instilled values in my sister and I that would stick with us for a lifetime, shaping me into the woman that I am today.

But I started feeling the weight of my parents' divorce at a young age. I felt the void of my dad not being home, and the reality that I didn't have a "normal" family life. I can remember being little and falling asleep holding my own hand, pretending it was my dad's. Every little girl needs a dad, and I was desperately feeling the lack of mine. My dad was still involved in my life and lived very close to us, but my family dynamic was still radically altered. I learned what it means to split holidays, time, and lives in a family due to divorce. Sometimes, it felt like I had two separate lives; that's when fantasy started to creep its way in.

I would dream about the future, but not in an exciting way that little girls should. I dreamed about it to escape the reality that I was currently in and created an entirely new scenario for myself, envisioning the future later on of how my life could be filled with happiness. I would dream, even as a little girl, that someone would want nothing more than to be with me, and then I wouldn't feel abandoned. It was safer that way living in another reality where I could create my own story and control the ending. I would escape there often in my mind, living for the future while not knowing how to remain and enjoy the present.

During all these new transitions in my life, I had started praying for my mom and dad to get back together. After about two years had passed since the divorce, I decided that maybe I should change my prayer, since what I was praying for clearly wasn't happening. Was God even listening? Did He care that I was hurting? Did He not want my family to get back together? I didn't understand. As I increasingly got more upset that my prayers weren't working, I changed my mind about what I should be praying for. I don't know how I knew to start praying for peace, except that I believe now the Lord placed that desire on my heart. So, I started praying for peace every night, truly having no idea what that even meant or what it would do in my life.

I don't remember how much time had passed, but one day, I woke up and something felt different. I realized for the first time, since hearing my parents say they were getting a divorce, I was going to be ok. I felt what I could only describe as warmth embracing me, like a tight hug from a friend you haven't seen in a long time. Have you ever sat by a warm fire on a winter night, a blanket wrapped over you, the cackling of the fire in the background as you lightly close your eyes and listen to loved ones around you talk? That feeling of rest right before you are about to enter a deep sleep? A calmness that comes over your entire body, reassuring you that you are safe here? It felt like all those things, only sweeter somehow.

I felt like a large, weighted blanket was covering me, but the blanket was a blanket of rest, ease, and reassurance. It somehow felt like it was enveloping me, drawing me close. There was a tangible presence of weight that it came with, like trying to move out of it would feel unnatural. But at the same time, my spirit and body felt lighter. "Come to me, all you, who are weary and burdened, and I will give you rest. Take my yoke upon you and learn from me, for I am gentle and humble in heart, and you will find rest for your souls. For my yoke is easy and my burden is light" (Matthew 11:28-30).

I knew in that moment what I had been praying for was happening. At seven years old, I didn't know what the word peace meant, but I knew it was encountering me. It was tangibly happening to me.

How is that possible? I thought. I didn't know what I thought peace was, but I was unaware that it could become an experience, unaware peace could come so close.

This was my first encounter with the tangible presence of God, and, in a moment, I went from knowing about God to knowing God for myself. His presence became so personal to me as He stepped into my pain and met me in the middle of it. He met a need when I was feeling abandoned and confused. From that moment on, no one could convince me that there wasn't a God. Jesus became so real to me that day, as I realized the person of Jesus is alive and cares enough to meet me where I was at.

Now, this didn't mean I didn't grieve anymore what had happened to my family, but I knew now that I could have peace in the middle of a storm. That I was never truly alone, as I had a reality to cling to that was bigger than my circumstances.

And that peace? It came often. I would pray most nights for it to come and meet me again, and without fail, it always came. Second Thessalonians 3:16 says, "Now may the Lord of peace himself give you peace at all times and in every way." I knew Jesus heard me, and that truth forever changed my life.

How about you? When was the moment when you first experienced God's presence coming close to you? When He spoke to you for the first time? Go back to that memory and look at how God was pursuing you, speaking to you, meeting a need, answering a prayer, drawing you close to Him.

Some of you might not have a memory that comes up because you didn't grow up with faith, or you've felt distant from God for a long time. But the beautiful thing is that if pursuit comes from God first, it's not dependent on whether you believed and followed Him or not. There have been moments all throughout your life where God was pursuing you. Ask Him to open your eyes and make you aware of the reality of that truth.

And if you're still struggling to see Him in your story, that's ok. My hope is that by the time you reach the end of this book, you will see the hand of God moving throughout your life.

That you would see the tangible reality of a God who pursues you and always has been.

But for now, read these following verses, and be encouraged in knowing your story of God's pursuit over your life started well over 2,000 years ago and is even recorded in the Bible!

"We love because he first loved us." (1 John 4:19)

"Surely your goodness and unfailing love will pursue me all the days of my life, and I will live in the house of the Lord forever." (Psalm 23:6 NLT)

LIGHT IN THE DARKNESS

("Rescue": Lauren Daigle)

THE NEXT FEW YEARS WERE QUITE A BLUR TO ME. I'VE LEARNED since being in therapy that when you go through something traumatic, it is normal for your brain to dissociate in a lot of ways because it is trying to protect itself. I don't want to, in any way, make it out that I had a horrible life because I didn't. I had a mom who loved us kids more than anything and supported us. We went on vacations every year and had a good home life. I was getting an education, I had friends, and I had a room of my own. There are a lot of good memories of my life. However, for the sake of my story, I'm choosing to tell the memories most prevalent to my pain because those are the ones that highly influenced the way I thought and lived at that current time in my life.

My relationship with my dad at that point in my life wasn't the healthiest, and it took a massive toll on me. I was hurt, confused, and incredibly insecure from the divorce. That didn't mean we didn't have fond memories together; we had a lot of fun moments with one another, and my dad always knew how to put smiles on our faces. Whether it was coming up with silly games for us to play or making us laugh with his outgoing, talkative nature, we shared many of those sweet memories together. And my dad was a present dad, which I am extremely thankful for. He showed up to every game my sister and I had and was even my basketball coach. But there was never any talk of what was really going on, of how I was emotionally doing. My voice didn't feel welcomed to explain my emotions, so silence became my weapon. I started telling myself that if I didn't speak up to how I felt, it would be a good day. If I didn't voice my opinion, or speak what was on my mind, then everything would be ok. I subconsciously taught myself that silence was key, so this bright, bubbly girl who used to love the spotlight slowly became more and more distant, shy as all heck, and anxious around people.

I know now that my dad loved me as best as he knew how during that time of his life, but he hadn't fully surrendered his life to Jesus at this point, so a lot of how he reacted came from places of hurt, pain, and anger. I craved attention and love, but I couldn't get it from someone who hadn't found it yet for himself.

As a young girl, I craved attention from others, especially male figures, in order to try and get a need met that I felt wasn't adequately being met. Have you ever felt that desire to be seen and known by someone else? That if someone got to know more of you, the depths of who you are, maybe you would finally feel understood? Maybe that void of feeling misunderstood would finally go away?

It's normal to wrestle with the feeling of being misunderstood. At the core of who we are, the only one who could truly know the depths of us, the complexities that make up all facets of who we uniquely are, is our Creator. Those questions posed above can lead us into the depths of who God is and who He made us to be when we ask them in light of searching for Him.

When we ask them apart from Him and try to fill those voids in our own ways, it can lead to some pretty dark places we never thought we'd end up in.

For some, trying to fill that void can turn into drinking, partying, drugs, etc. Other times, it might not look as "dark" externally, but internally you are struggling to fill a void by this obsessive need to please people, striving for perfectionism in everything you do, constantly trying to prove your worth in the things you accomplish, the money you make, etc.

All of our crutches look different, but the basis is the same. We are all yearning to feel understood, known, and loved. For me, my crutch, or attempt to fill in that void, is something I fell into, and slowly, over the years, had to stumble my way out of.

Somewhere along the way of craving attention from others, I stumbled upon pornography. I couldn't tell you the first re-collection of that memory or how it happened, but it became something that I occasionally watched, the youngest re-collection I can recall began around ten years old, to something that, along with masturbation, slowly started to consume me. I would spend hours a day pretending I was doing something else on my laptop when I was really just watching pornography. I would stay up for hours at night, consumed by images that I had seen. Now, I get you might read this and think how disgusting and sick that is. And I agree, but it's what I knew as a little girl to cope with the pain I didn't know I was suppressing. It became my view of what love looked like, what I thought was the picture of being deeply known and loved and vulnerable. It became an outlet for the pain, to feel something, anything, and I didn't realize yet what it was stemming from. So, I continued watching it, letting myself feel some kind of connection, climax, anything to feel pleasure just for a second before my world would go numb again.

I didn't have much hope. I felt defeated due to a lack of being connected to my own emotions and pain, and lived for any attention that any boy would give me. It used to really bother me when people would say, "Well, you don't do drugs or smoke or even really drink alcohol: you're so pure." Because pure was the farthest thing from what I felt. My sin and addiction were hidden, locked away in the depths of the darkest places, as I tried hard to never slip or let it be known that I was broken. But inside, I was screaming for help, just not necessarily knowing the words to use to let someone know. I can remember putting myself in the most degrading situations, instances now that it still shocks me sometimes how that used to be me. I was the object of men's sexual desires, and I knew it. But I craved connection and affirmation so much that I clung on to whatever was given to me.

I didn't know my identity or my worth yet, because my relationship with God wasn't secure in this season of my life. When you don't know how priceless you really are, you make a lot of dumb decisions along the way because you're not operating in the fullness that you were created for. Thank God (literally) that He's the best at turning ashes into beauty! (We'll get into this more later.) Honestly, I need to write a whole book about this time at some point to really do it any justice, but I'll talk a little more about the root and effects that pornography had on me later on in the book, since it's such a massive part of my story.

During that time, I entered high school and enjoyed my freshman year, well most of it, as I ended up getting diagnosed with scoliosis at the end of that year. That meant my spine had a curve that wasn't normal, and they needed to do something about it so that it wouldn't get worse later on in life. I was given a hard brace to wear, which started from right underneath my boob and ended right above my jean line. It consumed the entire front side of my body and velcroid in the back. You could literally knock on my stomach because the brace wasn't a soft cast. And the best part? I had to wear this beautiful accessory for 21-23 hours a day, even when I was sleeping, all throughout my sophomore year of school and some of my junior year as well. I was told that this cast wouldn't make my spine any better but would just prevent it from getting worse.

My mom and I went shopping to get all new clothes after getting the brace because I insisted on baggier and more over-sized clothes so that no one would know I was wearing this cast. I think about that now and realize how damaging of a mindset that was. My only concern was hiding, not wanting to show the real me, and hiding away in the shadows as much as I could. But even that was hard. I couldn't hide enough at school, so I refused to go. I would miss the bus and come tardy to school more times than I can count. By the grace of God, I passed freshman year, though the school informed me that my tardies were basically enough to fail me for the year. My dad would have to drive to my house in the morning, which was always a crying, screaming fight with my mom and I that she would call him to take me to the one place I didn't want to be. Once there, I would try to stay hidden as much as possible; God forbid anyone found out I was cast girl, as I called myself. It doesn't seem as big of a deal now, but back then in high school, it was the worst possible situation I could've imagined, or so I thought.

Have you ever been thrown a major curveball? Like it came so far out of left field that you never even saw it coming, and the wind seemed to get knocked out of you? I had a left field curveball moment that year on top of everything else I was already going through. It's still something really personal to me and isn't something I feel like I can write in here, so without going into details, I experienced something that year that I didn't see coming. It knocked the wind right out of me, and I felt completely blindsided. It also altered a lot of things in my life mentally and still isn't something I've fully been able to wrap my head around or reconcile with, but I know that there is more healing and redemption coming from it. I share this to say that my sophomore year wasn't a walk in the park; I hadn't expected anything that I experienced that year. Life can be like that sometimes, and it's in those moments that we see the foundations or lack therefore that we have built our lives on.

Why am I telling you all of this, you might ask? Sounds like a pretty depressing backdrop for this life story, huh? Well, I want to paint a picture for you, and I hope that through this painting, you're painting your own in your mind. I'm painting a picture of the things that were out of my control, the things that I did that really messed me up, and the things that hurt me. To see the glory in the story, you need to first see what it was before I surrendered it. My hope is that we can take a closer look at the gospel in our lives and see the stark difference of a life without Jesus and a life with Him.

It doesn't mean that everything is all of a sudden perfect, but your perspective changes, your view shifts, and your chains of bondage are broken. I'm hoping that as I share the really dark moments of my life by being transparent with you, you would be able to see the grace of God's goodness as this story continues to unfold. That you would see the heart of a loving Father relentlessly pursuing me and continuing to do so now. And that you would have a fresh revelation of His heart of pursuit for you as you continue to read.

Okay, so let's be clear: at this point in my life, I for sure believed in Jesus because I had experienced Him before. But as far as having a personal relationship with Him went, that was pretty much non-existent. I stopped attending youth group later into my high school years, because I just wasn't feeling connected to my faith or honestly cared enough to learn more. I talked about Jesus like I knew Him, but I truly didn't know Him at all. I lived with way more fear than peace and way more sin than right-eousness.

Sophomore year was that year when it seemed like the whole world just happened to be against me, and everything just felt like it was adding to the fire. I've heard that there is always a light at the end of a tunnel, but sometimes you can't see it, and sometimes it's not enough just to have it at the end. I've since realized something else. It's not just about seeing a light at the end of the tunnel; it's about seeing it right in the middle of the tunnel. I'm reminded of the tunnel in Connecticut we would always drive through as a kid. It's a long tunnel, and there is an orangish light all on the inside. As a kid (ok, honestly, I still do it), whenever I drove through it, I would yell out "ORANGE TUNNEL" before holding my breath until we made it out the other side. I would hold my breath, restricting the very oxygen I needed to breathe, in order to get out of the very location I was in and out to the other side. As soon as I was out of the tunnel, I would breathe a sigh of relief, letting all the air out and breathing in fresh new air.

I feel like we typically treat life like this. We hold our breath through the things that are unknown, the moments where we can't always see the light at the end of the tunnel. We try to power through to make it out the other side, but instead of coming out thriving, we come out gasping for new breath. We are so focused on the outcome, on reaching the destination, that we disregard the light inside of the tunnel. We try to fill the voids ourselves, barely surviving, when the light, Jesus, has been there the whole time, waiting to fill those voids for us. And in turn, we suffocate while in the tunnel, just trying to make it out alive. So often, we come out of pain, trauma, and being misunderstood just barely holding on. We're breathing though, right? So, we must be doing something right, we tell ourselves. We carry on in this independent state, thinking foolishly that we can mend our own broken wounds and insecurities, until we reach the next tunnel, hold our breath, and come out gasping once more.

Sometimes, I wonder what my life would've looked like if I realized sooner that there was a light inside the tunnel with me. That I wasn't meant to just get through, but I was actually made to thrive in the middle of the tunnel. That I could have deep peace and rest while driving through the difficult time.

That there was another option to take away the numbness I felt, and if I allowed myself to not rush through the tunnel, to not be so quick to suppress the pain, I would've seen another light in there with me, already creating a redemption plan to use it for my good and His glory. I would've seen the sovereign hand of God leading me to healing. I would've seen the pursuit of Jesus, waiting to heal those broken pieces and sitting with me in my pain, grieving with me.

I wish I had known that "Jesus wept" (John 11:35 NLT).

He weeps with me and feels deeply with me. He understands me. He understands you. I was never alone in any tunnel I faced in that time, and you are never alone in any dark tunnel you face. Whether it was something happening that was out of your control, like divorce or a scary diagnosis, or something you struggled with or are currently struggling with, like pornography, be encouraged that He never leaves you. Deuteronomy 31:6 reminds us of this when it states, "So be strong and courageous! Do not be afraid and do not panic before them. For the Lord your God will personally go ahead of you. He will neither fail you nor abandon you." I know that now, but I didn't then. What's crazy to me is that the verse in John mentioned above comes out of the context of Lazarus dying, one of Jesus's best friends. Jesus was going to resurrect him, but He still allowed Himself to grieve and to see the pain of the people who also loved Lazarus and missed him. Jesus wasn't quick to dismiss it and get through it. And we see the outcome one verse later in John 11:36 NLT: "Then the Jews said, 'See how he loved him!'" The love of Jesus was made known to people because of the way He let Himself be seen feeling deep pain and grief. Does that not blow your mind? Jesus didn't dismiss His own pain, but the people saw Jesus's love through that pain.

And the story didn't even end there. Lazarus was brought to life! I wonder what the people thought who were there experiencing this. For me personally, it would've shaken me to my core that Jesus raised this man from the dead but took time to allow Himself to feel pain before the miracle even came. He didn't try to rush to the good part of the story.

So often I feel like we try to rush to the "good" parts of our stories. But how would we live if we truly knew that Jesus was with us in our pain? That maybe He is more concerned with us being real with Him in the middle of it, and He will be faithful to get us through to the other side.

I also wish I knew the promise He had spoken to all of us in His word.

Isaiah 43:2-3: "When you pass through the waters, I will be with you; and when you pass through the rivers, they will not sweep over you. When you walk through the fire, you will not be burned; the flames will not set you ablaze. For I am the Lord your God, the Holy One of Israel, your Savior...."

This promise has since been a verse that has brought me so much peace and carried me through some really tough seasons.

He's the God who rescues you. Rescues you from sin, from insecurity, from not belonging. He understands you; He gets you. He sees the pain and emotions you don't know how to process. He sees that thing that was out of your control and has caused you pain, and He is waiting with open arms to heal that piece of your heart.

He saw the unjust things done to you and grieves with you the way a loving Father does. He sees the messes you've made and is still obsessed with you. He is and has been weaving together a story of redemption over those areas of your life and is relentlessly pursuing you to bring you into greater freedom. God goes to extreme measures to bring you freedom, confidence, and to show you that you've always belonged to Him. You are not some version of an extended family to Him but His immediate family. The ones He left heaven to get.

VICTORY IN THE BLOOD

("Victory is Yours": Bethany Wohrle and Bethel Music)

WE'RE GONNA SKIP PAST ALL THE AWKWARD BOYFRIEND STORIES, school dances, and girl sleepover stories in my life, though I had some fond memories of my high school years and some solid highlight moments. Senior year in high school was actually a pretty good year for me, with lots of fun moments that year, and I was excited for what the future held. My friends and I would find ways to leave and go out to lunch during school and figured out that we could come late into one of our classes if we brought the teacher Dunkin Donuts. We went on vacations with one another's families and had way too many phone calls and sleepovers to count! We boycotted the prom because all of us had broken up with our boyfriends (from the town next door), and they all somehow had gotten dates to our proms. So, we went to New York City instead for the day; it rained a ton, but we had the best day ever! These were the things that high school was made of for me, and I enjoyed every second of my senior year.

Senior year had a lot of memories that I hold fondly, but my senior class trip was not one of them. It was a day I looked forward to for a while, a whole day with my best friends, enjoying the last moments of our senior year before we went off to college in just a few short months. We planned our outfits, making sure we were picture-ready for all the photos we would take, making memories throughout the day. But that trip quickly turned into something I wanted to forget.

I was molested on that trip by a fellow student. After the incident, I stayed in bed for a solid two days where I couldn't do anything, as it left me feeling numb and powerless. I carried shame and guilt and didn't know how to tell my family about what had happened. I felt so much guilt as well because I had a boyfriend at the time when it occurred, and his response to what happened didn't help the situation either. I ended up going to the police about the incident at the urging of my friends. However, the whole situation was made public because my then-boyfriend beat the offender up the next day at school. This public outburst led to everyone finding out about my personal trauma, which was still new to me and triggering me daily. I can remember being asked questions, like "Why didn't you raise your voice, why didn't you say anything when it was happening?"

These questions only added on to the shame that I was already feeling. *Maybe they are right, maybe I should be held accountable for some of this,* I started to reason. But how many people know that when someone doesn't know their self-worth and doesn't really know they have a voice, it's almost near impossible to stand up and speak out when wrong is being done to them?

I can remember thinking, *I have no choice in what's happening; my voice doesn't matter, so I have to just hope that it ends soon.* The quiet word "no" or me pulling his hand away from my inner thighs were apparently not clear enough to show my intent. It was embarrassing that everyone at school knew and wasn't something that I wanted to be the center of attention for. I do remember though never regretting bringing the incident to the police.

It turned out that after I came forward, other girls came forward about similar experiences that had happened with them and this guy. Unfortunately, it would be two years until I would finally heal from what happened.

Trauma tends to be triggered when you don't know it is still there. It has a way of seeping into the cracks, and only when you're triggered do you see the broken sidewalk you've been walking on, a sidewalk that you thought had a better foundation than it did. That was more patched up than you thought. Trauma, when triggered, reveals the areas of your heart you've tried to tell yourself you've healed from but haven't yet. I didn't realize I was still hurting until I drove by the offender on a street a year later, and then two years later. My body tensed up at seeing him; everything went numb, and I would shake like crazy.

I'm going to say this next line because I believe someone probably needs to read it. I don't care that you could've say "no" more or louder when someone has hurt you. Your ability to word things correctly in a state of fear should never be the determining factor of how someone else gets to use your body for their benefit. Your inability to say things louder or stronger, or in a different manner, in a place of trauma doesn't give you permission to blame yourself for what occurred. I blamed myself for a while, thinking I should've done something different, but the fact of the matter is my body's reaction when I was confronted with the person who wronged me was fear. Your body responds to trauma that way, and no person should have to convince themselves that there was a better way to handle their trauma because no one should've ever put you in a place where your safety and consent was up for debate.

So, how could I confidently say Jesus relentlessly pursued me in the middle of abuse? In the middle of trauma, how is God still good? In the depths of pain, where was He?

That traumatic event was something I subconsciously chose to stuff down for the next few years. If I would've been honest with myself, I didn't see God in my pain. I felt like He abandoned me and was nowhere to be found. If you would've asked me, I would've said I was healed. When, in actuality, I had put a bandage of "time" over it and equated that with healing. Enough time had passed that I couldn't possibly still be triggered from that, or so I thought.

I realized that I was avoiding the hard questions. The questions I needed to confront of the guilt I felt toward myself for not speaking up, the hurt and anger I felt toward God for letting this happen to me. Only when I chose to confront the hard questions was I able to extend forgiveness toward myself, to receive grace, and to eventually extend forgiveness toward my offender. Only when I chose to confront the pain I had suppressed was I able to see a new perspective. A God who grieves with me, who never wanted that to happen to me. Only when I was able to take down my walls just enough to ask God to meet me in the pain was I able to see that God cared so much about me that He sent His only Son, Jesus, to not just die for my sins but to die for the things that happened to me as well. The blood of Jesus didn't just cover your sin, but it paid for your freedom, in every aspect. It paid for your trauma, your pain, your hurt.

Your abuse hung up on that tree with Him.

Let that sink in for a second. The emotional, verbal, physical, spiritual, or sexual abuse you have faced was covered in the shedding of Jesus's blood. What does this mean for you today? This means that over 2,000 years ago, Jesus saw present-day you, filled with wounds from life, things that we can't always control that happen to us. And while I don't have the answers for everything, the truth is that we live in a fallen world, and harmful, sinful things still occur. But what I do know is what Psalm 34:18 (ESV) says, "The Lord is near to the brokenhearted and saves the crushed in Spirit."

"Weeping may stay for the night, but rejoicing comes in the morning" (Psalm 30:5).

There is forgiveness available for you, to let go of the shame and guilt you've let yourself walk in for too long, grace extended to stop holding onto the lie that any of it was your fault, and the mercy of God to meet you in the middle of your story.

He is the God who sits with you in the pain and doesn't rush you out of it. He is tender to your emotions and sees the ways in which it has crushed you. But He also reminds us of a better way, a way to freedom in Him. He reminds us that there is rejoicing in the morning. That there is a new day, a better day coming, a restoration happening when we choose to let Him in. Apart from the Healer, complete total healing is not possible. "He heals the brokenhearted and binds up their wounds" (Psalm 147:3).

Isaiah 43:2 states, "When you pass through the waters, I will be with you; and when you pass through the rivers, they will not sweep over you. When you walk through the fire, you will not be burned; the flames will not set you ablaze."

This speaks to the reality that with Jesus, the very thing the enemy meant to crush you with can be redeemed. The very waters that were supposed to drown you will not sweep over you. The very things the enemy tried to burn you with and keep you in bondage to is not too big for God to restore.

The relentless love of God was in pursuit of you even back then, knowing that the blood of His Son would set you free from the bondage of any trauma you might've experienced.

"But he was pierced for our rebellion, crushed for our sins. He was beaten so we could be whole. He was whipped so we could be healed." (Isaiah 53:5 NLT).

There is healing made available to you in the blood of Jesus. In what He did on the cross for you. I know this verse is speaking to sin specifically, but the part I love about it is where it says, "so we could be whole, so we could be healed." Wholeness is connected to your entire being. Jesus paid for your salvation to have eternal life with Him, but in that, it didn't just cover your sin. It covered all sin, meaning sin and injustice that was done to you. He paved a way to experience freedom from the things that were out of your control. He relentlessly pursued your emotional well-being when His blood spilled red for you.

You Have My "Yes"

("Yes and Amen": Housefires)

MY SENIOR YEAR WASN'T EXACTLY ENDING THE WAY I HAD thought, but I held onto the excitement I was feeling at the thought of college starting and a fresh change, focusing on something positive. I had made a list of the schools I wanted to apply to, including one of the top party schools in the country. If there was one thing I planned on doing, it was going to be having fun in college and having my "freedom." During this process of applying for colleges, my mom informed me that I needed to apply to a Christian college. "You don't need to go," she said, but she wanted me to at least apply to one. She believed that a Christian college would be the most beneficial to me but would never force me to go. I had to choose on my own, she said, while she prayed that God would lead me. She knew choosing a college was a very big deal and gave me two options, Messiah or Gordon College. I blurted out Gordon without any thought. I wanted to make sure she knew even though I was applying, I definitely wasn't going, so I reluctantly told her I would apply to make her happy, but I absolutely was not going to any Christian college.

Now at the time, I really never prayed about anything in life. The only thing I prayed about was where I was supposed to go to school, mostly because I was scared to make the wrong decision, so I prayed about it for months. My mom and I went down to the Carolinas to tour some colleges, and it was there that I knew I was supposed to attend Gordon. People would later ask me how I knew I was supposed to be at Gordon and how I heard God telling me to go. Well, remember my first encounter with Him when I was little? When His presence came in the form of peace, and it was the first time Jesus became so real to me. I knew what His deep peace felt like. As I prayed about which college to attend, whenever I would pray about Gordon, I had such a deep peace on it that I didn't have for any other college I visited or prayed about. Because I felt such peace with Gordon, I started praying more about it and realized that this was where I was supposed to go. So, I said yes to attending.

I honestly did not want to go. It sounds funny but I had such peace about the school; however, I definitely wasn't thrilled to go. I wanted to run away from the whole Christian thing, not toward it. But somewhere deep inside myself, I trusted Jesus enough to go. He showed me there was peace in that decision, and I knew what the opposite of peace felt like, so I figured I could trust He knew what He was doing. So, in the fall of 2013, I packed up my car and left for Wenham, Massachusetts, where I would be a freshman at Gordon College to start my college career.

I was confident that Gordon was where I was supposed to be, but I had no idea that this would be the place where God really started changing my life. I had no idea yet that when you say "yes" to Jesus, He does more than you could've ever imagined with that simple act of obedience. I started seeing for the first time in my life that maybe He really did have a bigger plan for me than I did for myself.

Jeremiah 29:11: "For I know the plans I have for you" declares the Lord, "plans to prosper you and not to harm you, plans to give you a hope and a future."

As Christians, we've reduced the verse above to a nice cookie-cutter response when someone is uncertain about what their lives hold or where they are going. We use it like a seal on an envelope to try to package and give closure to what someone is feeling. And what I've found is that oftentimes, when we quote this verse from Jeremiah, we leave it at that and don't really understand the weight of what this verse means. We're constantly asking ourselves, "What am I supposed to do with my life?" And other people are always asking us what our plan is as well. Why do you think there are so many self-help books focused on this very topic? Because people are created with a divine, internal knowing that they have a purpose, that there is something bigger to their lives than what they know. We tend to go to other measures to seek out what that purpose is, but Jesus Himself tells us in the Bible that He has a plan for our lives. So, if there's a plan for our lives and God said He holds it, then we actually need to go to Him to see what that plan is. There isn't enough self-help books or inner soul-searching that can show you what your purpose is, so we must go to the source Himself to discover that truth.

A lot of times people quote Jeremiah 29:11 but stop reading after that verse in the Bible. It sounds like a nice, little bumper sticker verse, but if you keep reading more of Jeremiah 29, Jesus actually shows us how that plan will be revealed to us through the prophet Jeremiah's words. Oftentimes, we want the plans without the One who created them involved. But the plans for your life without the Creator are just plans; it's only when He continuously breathes on them that they come to life. If you're into the self-help kinda books to discover your purpose, the next verse to follow is Jesus's version of that. He practically shows us what it looks like to know the plans He has for our lives.

"Then you will call on me and come and pray to me, and I will listen to you. You will seek me and find me when you seek me with all your heart. I will be found by you, declares the Lord, and will bring you back from captivity." (Jeremiah 29:12-14)

His plan is actually a promise. His plan for your life is that you will know Him. That you will seek Him. I believe that your calling, your destiny, and His plan are revealed in this very verse mentioned above. We were born with a unique purpose and destiny that He placed inside every single one of us beforehand. For some of us, that might look like being a youth group leader, a CEO of a company, a doctor, a teacher, a mother, a father, etc. But more than anything we do or any title we have, we are His. Jesus's plan is that we will seek Him with everything we have, and His promise is that when we do, we will find Him and know Him intimately.

Sometimes we treat our purpose for our lives as something we really have to search high and low for. But if it's already placed inside of us, then our responsibility is more so about discovering what it is rather than searching for it. So, how do you discover it? By seeking the One who created it. And as you seek God, He says He will restore you from being a captive to this world, to living in the freedom you were created to live in. Your purpose and call are so engrained in your DNA, becoming who you are and how He created you, so you don't need to go off looking for it. God promises that as we seek Him, He will bring us back from captivity and into the fullness of who He created us to be.

So, what is captivity? It is a state of bondage that we were never supposed to be in. This could look like obvious sin, like partaking in drugs, drinking in excess, sexual sin, etc. It could also look like bondage in our thoughts: living from a place of constantly needing to people-please, feeling like we are never good enough, and believing lies about ourselves that are simply not how God sees us. It could look like living a life consumed by anxiety and depression. Whatever that bondage is for you, Jesus wants to bring us back to our original state of being.

But what is our original state? It's the freedom we were created to live in, the fullness of who we are. So, when we seek God, He breaks off captivity, the sin and lies that we've become entangled in, revealing to us who He is in us and who He created us to be. We only can know the plan for our lives as we become like the One who holds the plan, as the verse from Jeremiah states. God takes the weight off everything that we've taken hold of that we weren't meant to deal with, from sin to trauma to lies we are living by. He releases us from captivity, bringing us back to our original states where He uniquely expresses Himself through us and the purpose and calling He's placed inside of us.

I share all this because I really started searching for God while in college. It wasn't much at first, but I wanted to know Him more. And as you go on this journey with me, as more of my story unfolds, you'll see that I was filled with purpose when I sought Him, especially when He broke the chains of captivity I was under.

Yes, I did seek Him, but He started pursuing my heart long before I was ever curious to know Him. I could only choose Him in return because He first chose me. I think back to my mom even telling me I needed to apply to one Christian college. Without her insisting that I do that, I wouldn't have done that on my own. I wouldn't be where I am today, spiritually. God was pursuing me and knew exactly where I needed to be for me to actually become more aware of Him working in my life and to seek Him more.

So, what do you notice about those verses above from Jeremiah? The first part is Him declaring to us that He has a plan, a purpose, a hope, and a future for us. The first part is Him saying He knows us and is pursuing us, while the second part of the verse is our response. He offers the abovementioned promise to us, telling us that He's got us, that He's with us, and that He's pursuing us. The next lines are an invitation to pursue Him back. Did you notice that He pursued first? That He chose us and had us in mind first? He chose us; we just get to say yes in return.

Second Corinthians 1:20 says, "For no matter how many promises God has made, they are 'Yes' in Christ. So, I echoed my "amen" back to the "yes" He had spoken over me, of where He was leading me. And so through him the 'Amen' is spoken by us to the glory of God." His "yes" is a declaration of His prom-ise, and as we utter back "amen," He floods us with more of Him. Your echo back to God is an agreement for what He's spoken over you. And as you seek more of Him, you see more of who He created you to be.

EVEN WHEN IT HURTS

("Even When It Hurts": Hillsong United)

WORSHIP HAS ALWAYS BEEN A BIG PART OF MY LIFE. I CAN REMEMBER even when I was in my darkest moments, where I wasn't quite sure what I believed about faith, about Jesus, I would find myself on my knees crying and worshiping Him. It's what I knew to do. I had never seen anyone worship the way in which I was worshipping alone, but it was the way I knew to respond to the Lord. And I truly believe that worship and the pursuit of the Lord kept me from completely walking away from Him. I didn't read my Bible, I didn't pray, but I knew that God was real: I just didn't know Him yet personally. I didn't know how good He actually is. How kind He is. How much freedom He gives.

My freshman year of college really overwhelmed me. I was attending a Christian college and going to Bible classes, but I didn't know any of the Bible stories, even though I grew up in the church. They were foreign to me, and I felt really left out in class. You're probably wondering how I could've grown up in the church and didn't know any of these Bible stories. We'll get to that a little later on in this chapter.

This part of my story is pretty personal, but I firmly believe in being authentic and real, not sugarcoating anything. This world is too used to sugarcoating things, and I spent a lot of my life doing that, so I'm not about it. Remember how I shared with you about my struggle with pornography and masturbation? Well, it had become a full-blown addiction at this point in my life. I would sit in my social work classes reading about addiction but couldn't see that I, myself, was battling with it. Addiction, simply put, is when you can't say no to something, and it consumes and has priority in your life, costing you more than you ever intended it to. It cost me time, peace, relationships, grades, honesty, trust, joy, sleep, my worth and value, my perspective on sexuality, and so much more.

So, why keep doing it, you ask? Addiction doesn't care about all the things you're losing. It preys on the weaknesses and highlights the climax, reminding you of its escape, even if only temporary. It starves you of everything you actually need and convinces you that what it offers is better. It eats away at everything that's good until you're left returning to it more starved than when you first faced it. Addiction's promises are fleeting, and when you realize addiction is nothing more than a liar, you're already trapped in the cycle with no way out.

Addiction tells you that it's someone else's problem, that you're not really that bad. I know we typically talk about these things and think of pornography as a man's issue, but ever since talking about it more openly, and researching it, I've come to find out how many women deal with this struggle as well. According to a survey done in 2020 by the Barna Research Group, 65% of millennial women say they view porn at least a few times a year. The website, Covenant Eyes, which aids in helping people to stop watching pornography, came out with statistics in 2018 in regard to the realities of porn use. They stated that the world's most popular porn site, Pornhub, reported in 2017 that there were 28.5 billion annual visits to their site alone, with 68 years' worth of content uploaded. Webroot Cybersecurity says that there are 40 million Americans regularly visiting porn sites. So, chances are, if you are reading this, you have either struggled personally with pornography, have seen it at least once before, or have someone very close to you who is dealing with this.

Again, this topic is such a massive part of my story, but it deserves a whole entire book on its own to really do it any justice, so we're just scratching the surface of it.

Any kind of sexual addiction completely takes over your mind as well. Whatever consumes your mind consumes your heart also. Matthew 6:21-22 says, "For where your treasure is, there your heart will be also. The eye is the lamp of the body. If your eyes are healthy, your whole body will be full of light." What I prioritized in my mind showed where my heart laid. And if your eyes are the lamp of the body, that means it's important to realize what you are viewing. If my eyes were being consumed by images that weren't pure, it's not a shock that I wasn't healthy. My whole body was paying a price for what I was allowing my eyes to see because it was affecting my heart.

Up until this point, not a single soul knew what I was dealing with. I did everything possible to keep it hidden because I felt so disgusting and ashamed about it. I can distinctly remember my sophomore year in college as being the worst year of my life in terms of how lost I felt. I was deeply hurting after a relationship, putting myself in horrible situations with other men that year while slowly starting to drink to cope. I was feeling lonely, depressed, and confused, like I didn't fit in anywhere. I sure as heck didn't fit in with the Christians at school, although I could put up a good front. But I didn't fully fit in with the other kids who were fully immersed in the party life either. I wasn't sold out to either lifestyle, and not knowing who you are makes it hard to find your people.

I knew that Jesus could offer me a better life, but I wasn't ready to give up everything I had. This truth is ironic because the very things that I had were the very things that were slowly killing me on the inside. However, I didn't want to be one of those Christians who was only half in; I knew that if I really was about to commit my life fully to Jesus, there was no turning back. I would be all in, but I wasn't ready to be all in yet. I wasn't ready to give up my way of life yet, because it was what was familiar and what I knew.

There was one morning when I went to chapel (we had chapel three times a week), and this particular day would be more impactful on me than I knew at the present time. My school would have different people come and speak at chapel throughout the course of the school year. I can recall that I was sitting on the left side on the first floor of the chapel when the woman on the stage started speaking and sharing her previous battle with pornography. It was the first time I had ever heard someone talk about pornography publicly, let alone a woman. She shared her story of freedom, and suddenly, the possibility of freedom became tangible to me. I had believed that I would most likely just live my whole life like this, because I didn't know that true freedom existed. What she shared in her speech gave me another option, another perspective on change. I made a deal with God that day. I told Him that if anyone ever opened up to me about their struggle with pornography, I would come clean with mine. Of course, I didn't actually think that was ever going to happen, but a deal's a deal.

I left sophomore year feeling broken and numb, feeling lost, purposeless, and just confused as to what I actually wanted in life. I can remember going home for the summer and planning out what my junior year was going to look like. I was going to drink and party, sleep around a ton, and just basically screw up my life. I didn't care about anything anymore. It was decided; I had my plan in place.

Sometime during the summer months of that year, God supernaturally orchestrated a friendship into my life with someone I didn't know would be the pivotal point for my start to healing. We went to a church service together, and when we hung out afterward, he ended up confessing to me that he struggled with pornography. I had never in all my life had someone share something so vulnerable with me. My heart began to pound as I recalled the deal I had made with God earlier that year, coming clean with my addiction if someone did so with theirs. I instantly was brought back to that pew on the left side of the chapel, where I had heard a woman's story of freedom only months prior. However, I couldn't do it; I couldn't share. I felt so convicted to share because of the promise I had made with God, but shame plagued me. I couldn't get my mouth to open up and speak out the truth of my own problem.

See, that's what sin does, telling you that you would be seen as disgusting, even when you have a person in front of you who understands the battle. Sin wants to tell you that you are the only one dealing with it, that no one else will understand the issue. But I learned something else profound about sin that night. Sin loves the darkness. It wants to stay in the dark because it knows that once it's exposed to the light, that's where true freedom is found. When it's hidden and alone, it can grow and fester in a person but when it's revealed, shame and guilt break off, truth is discovered, and freedom is let in.

Ephesians 5:13: "But everything exposed by the light becomes visible—and everything that is illuminated becomes a light."

Think about it this way: Let's say you have a kitchen and a living room right next to each other. If you turn on a light in the kitchen, when you walk into the living room, the light has most likely spilled over into that room as well. Even if you can't see super clearly in the living room, it's not nearly as dark as it was because there is a light on nearby. Bringing sin into the light is very much the same. When my friend exposed his addiction to me, my world still looked a little dim because I wasn't free from it yet. But all of a sudden, there was also some light in my world. I saw what was possible, as the light always offers an invitation for change. You can choose to step forward, or you can choose to deny the bit of freedom you saw and remain stuck. Light always offers a choice.

So, I chose to step forward.

I can remember in that moment confessing for the first time what I had struggled with for years. My body was shaking because I never actually believed that this moment would come. And do you know what? Darkness tried telling me that I would be met with judgement and ridicule. Fear tried to tell me that if I exposed my addiction, I would feel like nothing more than the very shame I was trying to get rid of.

But instead, I felt a burden lift off me. I could feel an actual weight removed from my shoulders, and it felt like I became lighter. I was met with support and words, such as, "You're so brave; I'm so proud of you; You are going to be completely healed from this." Those words encouraged me more than I even knew I needed to hear at the time.

Now let me preface this and say that it would be years before I received my full complete healing. That wasn't because God didn't want to heal me and make me whole, but I had a lot of heart stuff to work through before I received full healing. There are people I know of that have been set free from things in an instance. I fully believe in that and know that freedom is possible. However, my story looked different, as I had to walk through the depths of my addiction with Him. And wow, was He patient with me. He never gave up on my freedom, and He will never give up on your freedom. His son, Jesus, paid for it all on the cross, and He will pursue you with everything inside of Him to see that you receive this freedom and walk in it fully.

This was just the start of my healing journey.

So, back to why I didn't know any Bible stories when I started college. I can distinctly remember being a young girl. I'm talking about thirteen-year-old Allecia sitting in the pews for church and knowing that it was a time I could tune everything out. That part is not abnormal, as I'm sure lots of kids would regularly check out from the Sunday service message. But what was abnormal is that the entire time during service, it would be as if a pornographic screen was playing across my mind. Things that I had seen, images and videos, consumed my mind until it was time to leave the service.

Now, I understand that some of you reading this relate to this deeply while others are completely baffled, if not even disgusted, by what you're reading. And I hear you. I look back on it now and also think it's disgusting. Heck, I even thought it was then but was in denial so much that I, myself, was partaking in the very thing that made me angry. In writing this, I think what I want to be careful to do is not to dehumanize people when we read stories like this. It's fine to think that the act itself is disgusting, because it's not who we were created to be, but it's another thing to look at the person and attach that disgust on them personally. They are living in sin and hurt. Seeing sin for what it is actually where that righteous anger comes from, but it's never meant to be directed at the person themselves. When we direct that disgust at people, it prevents them from feeling they can come forth in transparency, making them feel stuck in a cycle they are unsure how to get freed from.

I learned a lot about this through the way Jesus confronted me about my addiction. I started to see Him in a different light because of the way He approached this with me. For so long, I thought He was angry and disappointed with me because of what I was doing in secret. I wouldn't talk to Him, pray, or read my Bible because I felt completely unworthy. I was in sin, and I knew it, so I ran as far away from God as I could. Thinking back on it, it makes me think of Adam and Eve. As soon as they sinned in the garden, the Bible states that shame entered in, and they hid from God rather than run toward Him. (Genesis 3:8)

It wasn't until after sophomore year of college, after I tried transferring out because I didn't want to be at Gordon anymore, that God met me in the middle of all of this once more. For a class assignment, I had to choose an addiction, write a paper on it, and then present it in one of my social work classes.

Ironically, I choose pornography. If that doesn't show you how much I was in denial of what I was battling, then I don't know what does. It's important to note that while I experienced a level of freedom from confessing my addiction to someone else, I hadn't made any active steps toward healing. I now see that what happened next was able to happen because God had met me previously in this area of difficulty. That He had been pursuing me in the area of freedom for quite some time. Oftentimes, there are a few steppingstones that lead up to more breakthroughs, and this was one for me.

Two days before the paper was due, I was in class and was filled with tremendous anxiety. I couldn't stop shaking, while my heart was pounding out of my chest. It carried on like this for two days. I felt like I was having a nervous breakdown and would have to excuse myself out of the classroom just to breathe. For some reason, every memory of ever feeling belittled, rejected, and/or degraded came flooding back to me. Everything I had ever done or watched or seen regarding pornography came racing back to the forefront of my mind, and the weight became unbearable. I didn't know yet that I was feeling the weight of my sin and the weight of the pain I had been stuffing down for so long. The weight of sin started becoming more real to me when I started confessing what was actually going on in my life. I honestly believe that writing that paper started to give me another glimpse into the freedom possible for me, though I didn't know how to get it yet.

I remember going back to my dorm the night before the paper was due, and I read through it once, focusing on how I would present it. Immediately, I started crying because it hit me that I had written a paper about myself. I can't tell you why it took that moment for it to click in my head, but it wasn't until I was reading something I thought was really distant from me before it hit home to me. Even though I had started confessing it to multiple people, I was in denial of the ways it had affected my life and the reality that I was still struggling deeply with addiction. I remember messaging my professor, telling her I couldn't present on my paper because it was way too personal and raw right then. Thankfully, she excused me from presenting it in class. It's the most surreal thing to be reading about something you've done so much research on that has brought bondage to so many people, only to see yourself staring back through the paper, realizing that the person you're reading about is you.

Around this time, I had become aware of what sex trafficking was and became very passionate about this issue. I even flew to Ohio for a week on my spring break to be a part of a program where I could learn more about it. There at the program, I learned how intricately woven pornography was to this industry, and it broke my heart that I was contributing to something I was so passionate about dismantling. That was another reason I distanced myself so far from the idea that I was still struggling. I didn't want to admit I was a part of the problem because it hurt too much.

That truth, mixed with the breakdowns I had been having for the past two days over the paper, became too much to handle. I cried out to God and told Him that I needed Him to take this addiction from me. Previously, I had heard of people saying before to "give things to God," but I didn't know how to do that. However, that approach became really simple to me that night.

I recognized I couldn't function like this anymore, as the weight of shame and guilt I felt were unbearable. I had nothing else to lose and was desperate to get rid of those feelings. I came to Him in my most broken state, hiding nothing, and asked Him to take all shame and guilt away. Miraculously, I can remember feeling a weight, again, physically lift off my shoulders, and from that day on, I never felt shame or guilt ever again around struggling with pornography and the situations I had put myself in. Even when I continued to mess up, which was a lot. Kris Vallotton, one of the pastors of Bethel Church, said the following in his book, *Supernatural Ways of Royalty*, "The blood didn't just cover our past mistakes; it covered all our moments of stumbling as we learn to live as free sons and daughters."

But I learned something really valuable about the nature of God in that moment. Previously, I had a view of a disappointed God, sitting up in heaven looking down upon me. But afterward, I started to understand that He was a loving Father who wasn't afraid to get in messes with His kids. He stooped low to where I was and met me right in the middle of my mess.

If there's currently any mess you are in, I want to say from someone whose been there that God is right in the middle of it with you. You are never too far gone. Jesus is not looking at you as someone who needs to be fixed, but rather someone who He can't wait to make whole. Your freedom came with a price, but it was worth Him hanging on a cross to take it back for you. He does not take your freedom lightly. Too many people walk around thinking that true, full freedom is for when they arrive in heaven. But Jesus came to bring heaven to earth. "Your Kingdom come, your will be done, on earth as it is in heaven" (Matthew 6:10). He didn't just pay to get you into heaven one day; He paid to get heaven inside of you right now.

If there's anything that you are scared to bring to the light, spend a few minutes right now confessing it to Jesus. Call up someone you trust and share it with them. Don't just carry on reading this book if you resonate with this. Sit with Jesus for a few minutes and hand the struggle over to Him. Some of you will be set free of immediate shame and guilt in an instant, and others will begin the process of the healing journey that will take time. But know that whatever happens, God's with you in every step. Your healing journey could begin right now. Let Him into the deepest parts of your heart to help you heal.

There's A Third In The Trinity

("Starts and Ends": Hillsong United and Touch of Heaven: Hillsong United)

It was 2016, and I was attending Hillsong Church in New York City. The former pastor, Carl Lentz, mentioned that the true essence of our faith is when we get on our knees and seek heaven for ourselves.

We're a generation that likes to be spoon-fed, whether we want to agree with that sentiment or not. We are all about the quick fix, the next cool thing, the fastest most efficient way to get something, etc. I mean, think about it. Have you ever noticed yourself getting frustrated that your phone doesn't seem to quite be working at the speed you want it to? The normal five seconds to click to a new page online is prolonged to more than thirty, and you notice yourself clicking the screen repeatedly, telling the "stupid thing" to work. No, just me? Great.

Funny enough though, this isn't actually how we're initially wired. Let's go back to Jeremiah 29:13 again briefly.

"You will seek me and find me when you seek me with all your heart."

A lot of people want to know God but aren't willing to spend time getting to know Him. A lot of people are curious to know more about the Creator and the answers to life that He holds but are just as quick to back away when those results don't come fast enough. We approach Jesus in a, "What can you do for me" mentality, "how can I benefit, what will you give me?" He already did abundantly more than you or I will ever be able to adequately thank Him for, paying a price that none of us could pay. He could've stopped right there, showing us the way into eternal life with Him, and that alone would be enough reason to worship Him for the rest of our lives. But He is not the God of "just enough." He is the God of more than enough, as it is His nature to give out of abundance. So, He will meet us over and over again when we seek Him, because He's that good and patient.

Our focus needs a radical shift in the way we view worship. Are we worshipping the things He promises us or how we will benefit from them, or are we actually worshipping the King of Kings for everything He's already done, for the very nature of who He is as Redeemer, Healer, Protector, Lover, etc.? What does worship mean to us? What does adoration mean to us?

Let me go back to the phrase I mentioned earlier by Pastor Carl Lentz. I believe that there are so many people who haven't gotten before the Lord and sought Him for themselves. We rely on other people, on church, a pastor, a friend who is a Christian, a mentor, etc., for help. We have questions, but we typically look everywhere else for them besides the One who holds the answer. Those things, in and of themselves, aren't bad, but in our searching, we must also go to the Source Himself.

I say all this because I attended a Christian college, and if I'm being honest, the majority of that campus, myself included, needed a radical shift in perspective of our faith. We needed a radical shift in what the gospel meant, in what Jesus actually did for us on the cross. We were well- intentioned people who I believe genuinely wanted to know more about the faith we confessed but were sold something short of what the gospel really is and what relationship with Jesus really looks like. I would see myself not living in the freedom I believed was accessible and started thinking that there had to be more to my faith. More to this God I followed.

I didn't understand why my Christian campus looked like campuses that weren't Christian, in terms of the lifestyles we were living, the lack of freedom we lived in, and the overall lack of pursuit for Jesus. John 17:16 says, "They are not of the world, even as I am not of it." Jesus taught us that we weren't supposed to look like the rest of the world, that true Christians would live radically different from people who didn't believe in Him. What I saw at my college campus was the opposite.

There was a confrontation of choice occurring. This wrestling and unsettledness within me to crave something deeper than just attending church on Sunday. I wrote this on January 29, 2019, a few years after I had graduated college, but I think it explains well the reality that a lot of people within the church are experiencing.

The other day, I laid down on the chairs in worship, flat on my face, just truly wanting nothing but Him. I am not interested in hype Christianity. Hype Christianity doesn't require you to lay down your life for the King of Kings. It is based on feelings. Hype Christianity lasts for a little while, but when you are forced to examine your walk with the Lord, you realize that you cultivated nothing. You were left with a false representation that you had a deep friendship with Jesus.

I understand that entry might be heavy to read, but I was starting to have this realization that there had to be more to Christianity than what I was seeing around me. If my life was so precious that it was worth someone dying for it, was I living in everything that He paid for? Did Jesus die for me to be living the way I was living, or was there more to this Christianity thing than I knew? So many people around me were caught up in sexual immorality, shame, fear, depression, anxiety, etc. Most of these people attended church every week, would hear a nice sermon, feel good during worship, and carry on with the rest of their week without anything changing about the way they lived life. There had to be more freedom than this. There had to be more to this life.

Have you ever hooked up with someone where getting with them was the only intention in mind? Where the chase of finally getting to be with them satisfied a desire to feel connected? Bear with me for a second. I, in no way, am condoning this, but in my past when I would do this, I would hype up the moments leading up to that with my friends.

You hype yourself up beforehand, going into it with the intentions of how you will benefit and coming out of it still hyping up the ways in which you benefited.

It's all about the hype, with no commitment to the other person. It's all about what you can get, not what you can give.

I started noticing that most people in the church, again myself included, weren't too far off from this idea. There has been a culture created around feelings, idolizing ways in which you can benefit, of what following Jesus can do for you. While it is true that Jesus changes your life for the better, we don't follow Him because of what He could do for us. We follow Him because of what He has already done for us. With this first belief, as the core foundation of a lot of people's faith, came a lot of people who said yes to giving their lives to Him, good- intentioned people who really had no idea of what that actually meant.

We were a people sold out to hype instead of Jesus Christ. We were a people who didn't know how to seek Him for ourselves and cultivate our own relationships with Him. We were a people that unknowingly, unwillingly became about the hype of the idea of Jesus rather than a committed people to the person of Jesus.

I took a look around at the Christianity that I saw and said, "If this is all there is to it, then this isn't worth me giving my whole life to God." I knew that there had to be more, whatever that meant, and I told myself that if I found that more, I would be all in. I would give my life fully to Jesus and promised Him that I wouldn't just be someone who talked about it but would live out whatever Christianity was intended to be. If I found that Christianity was more than I was told or seeing, whatever that looked like, I would pursue Him to the ends of this earth. This was a big deal to me, because if you know me, you know that when I'm passionate about something, I am all in. There is no backing out or giving up. I was willing to serve Jesus for the rest of my life, even if it didn't look like anything else around me. If I found the more that I was searching for, I would run with it at full force and was willing to pay whatever cost to find it.

So I went back to my roots: worship. The only thing I knew to do in moments like this. I can remember driving my car around at night during my college years and parking it in random places, churches, streets, schools, and just crying out to God. I would blast my worship music with tears streaming down my face, as I was desperate for more of Him. You see, the thing is I had had very real encounters with Him before, and those encounters showed me that there was more to Him than what the church was telling me. That there was more than what my college was telling me. That there was more than what Christians were telling me. I was so desperate for Him to show up in my life even more so that I would do this regularly driving with worship music playing, waiting for Him to show up. I didn't know what I was waiting for and what the "more" I was searching for included. I didn't know how long I would cry out before He would meet me, but I knew I wouldn't stop. Instead, I'd come back time and time again, sometimes walking away filled with hope and other times driving away feeling as if He wouldn't ever show up more than what I had already previously seen.

And here's what I found out when you start searching. If the promise is that you will find God when you seek Him, then in order for Him to reward that, He has to actually place the desire inside of you.

Think about it this way: If a child isn't eating their veggies, their mom might say to them, "I promise I will give you your favorite dessert if you are a good boy tonight and eat all your veggies." What did you notice? The only way it is possible for the boy to know he will be given his favorite dessert is because the promise was spoken to Him.

He is let in on the promise, as it is not hidden or kept a secret from him.

And when his mother releases that promise, the young boy now knows what is possible, and he has an inner desire to finish the food before him because he knows his mom is true to her word.

God does the same thing with us. He initiates the promise, fueling us with a desire so that He will give what He promised us. He sets the expectancy, lets you in on how to get more of Him, you run toward it by seeking, and He continues to fuel the desire in you until you see the promise fulfilled. Desperation stirs the hunger; hunger fans the flame; and His glory rests within the flame. Where there is fire, there our God is also.

Did you know that it is actually impossible to fuel your own hunger to desire more of the Lord? It was my hunger that kept bringing me back, over and over again, to a place where I would cry out for God to come and touch my life. But He placed the desire in me first. "For no one can come to me unless the Father who sent me draws them to me, and at the last day I will raise them up" (John 6:44 NLT). It is the pursuit of your heavenly Father that delights in drawing you to Himself first. He makes

Himself accessible by drawing you near to Him. It is in the very core of your being that you have an innermost desire to be known by the Creator of the Universe and to know Him, because you were made in His image. "So God created human beings in his own image. In the image of God he created them; male and female he created them" (Genesis 1:27, NLT)

The song I mentioned in the beginning of this chapter, "Starts and Ends" by Hillsong United, starts off with lyrics talking about your soul thirsting for things you aren't able to explain, and a deep desire in your very being to pray.

There was an inner cry of my heart that was starting to be released at that time. Every single person's soul thirsts for things they can't comprehend. Inside every human being is an innate desire to be known and loved, to seek answers to the questions they can't begin to wrap their minds around.

In the book of Matthew, it is written, "Blessed are those who hunger and thirst for righteousness, for they will be filled" (Matthew 5:6).

Who carries righteousness? God does, because He Himself is the very definition of righteousness. "For the Lord is righteous, he loves justice; the upright will see his face" (Psalm 11:7). So, this verse in Matthew is saying that those who hunger and thirst for God Himself will be satisfied by Him.

Then three books later, in John 6:35, we see Jesus say the following statement: "I am the bread of life; whoever comes to me will never go hungry, and whoever believes in me will never be thirsty."

What can you gather from these verses? Hunger is actually a cycle. Thirst is actually a cycle. First, we see that those who are satisfied are those who hunger and thirst for Jesus. How can you hunger and thirst for Him? Like we saw in Genesis 1:27 above, God created man in his own image. Every single person on this earth was made in the likeness of God. But not only were we made in His likeness, but we have the breath of the Almighty One in us. Genesis 2:7 says, "Then the Lord God formed a man from the dust of the ground and breathed into his nostrils the breath of life, and the man became a living being." We are the only creatures on this earth that the Lord God breathed into, giving us life.

John 1:1 says: "In the beginning was the Word, and the Word was with God, and the Word was God." He took the very essence of who He was and breathed it into us, to where the Word now dwells within us. The breath of life breathed the very Word of God into us, making us in His likeness that we would long for Him and desire Him above all else. That we would be able to have deep communion and fellowship with the Creator of the Universe.

So, what can we gather from all of this? No one is left out. Every single person has the same opportunity to seek His face. Since we were all created in His likeness, and the breath of God has been breathed into every one of us, we all have an innate desire to be deeply known and to know the Creator. It is in our blood, actually breathed into our very DNA.

You were made to hunger and thirst for God, and as you do, His promise is that He will fill you up so that you will never hunger and thirst for the things that this world offers. Instead, you will be overflowing with the water of life that only He can give.

John 4:14 says, "But those who drink the water I give will never be thirsty again. It becomes a fresh, bubbling spring within them, giving them eternal life" (NLT).

So, there I was, on my quest to find more of Jesus, when I was invited to a ministry retreat. My best friend and roommate for the first two years of college, Miski, was helping to lead a ministry group on campus, and the leaders from the group were having a small retreat at her house for the weekend. I wasn't a part of the ministry at all, but she invited me to come anyway. I can remember that night so clearly. I had said yes to going, but I actually was kind of dreading it. I really didn't know anyone, and it was snowing out like crazy that weekend. A real typical Nor'easter. The thought of cozying up in my bed for the night started to sound much more appealing. After much hesitation, the leaders decided to drive the hour-and-a-half trip to my friend's house in New Hampshire, despite the frigid weather and warnings of a snowstorm on top of the snow we already had. I reluctantly walked down the hill with my bags and made it to the chapel where we were all meeting. Of course, only after face-planting in the snow on the way down the hill. I thought, *So, this is how this weekend is going to go.* Solid.

Have you ever had one of those moments in your life that you look back on, thinking, *Wow, if only I knew how much my life was going to change in that present moment?* This weekend was one of those times for me. It's a weekend I look back on, seeing how much my life was impacted by this sole weekend. I had absolutely no expectancy for anything; gosh, I didn't even want to be there, and still, Jesus met me right in the middle of it.

Miski had this woman that she knew come over to her house who she had been family friends with for a while. The group of us who had come on this retreat, including this woman, spent a long time just worshipping in the living room. She then asked if there was anyone who had not yet been baptized in the Holy Spirit.

I remember thinking, *Well, I'm pretty sure that's me because I have no idea what she's talking about.* I had heard about it once from Miski, and I remember distinctly thinking, *I have no idea what that is, but if it's you, Jesus, then I want it.* What I would later find out is that Miski had been praying two months for me for the baptism of the Holy Spirit before this retreat night.

We could spend a whole book alone going through the baptism of the Holy Spirit but if you want to read more, you can check out one, or all, of the following books from trusted people of faith:

- *How to be Filled with the Holy Spirit*, A.W. Tozer
- *Baptized in the Spirit: God's Presence Resting Upon You With Power*, Randy Clark
- *The Holy Spirit Baptism*, Reinhard Bonnke

The Holy Spirit dwells within you for your sake. Every believer that accepts Christ into their lives has the Holy Spirit dwelling within them. We are then able to live holy lives and walk in greater freedom because of conviction and the ongoing sanctifying power of the Holy Spirit in us. The baptism of the Holy

Spirit though enables believers to walk in the power that God has poured out on them to be His witnesses and allows them to walk in ministry supernaturally.

Acts 1:4-5: "On one occasion, while he was eating with them, he gave them this command: 'Do not leave Jerusalem, but wait for the gift my Father promised, which you have heard me speak about. For John baptized with water, but in a few days you will be baptized with the Holy Spirit.'"

Notice the difference in the next two verses. Acts 2:38 says, "Peter replied, 'Repent and be baptized, every one of you, in the name of Jesus Christ for the forgiveness of your sins. And you will receive the gift of the Holy Spirit.'" And then Acts 1:8 says, "But you will receive power when the Holy Spirit comes on you; and you will be my witnesses in Jerusalem, and in all Judea and Samaria, and to the ends of the earth.'" One verse describes the Holy Spirit as a gift dwelling within when you receive salvation. Another describes the baptism as the Spirit coming upon you for the sake of power.

I'll give ya one more verse to consider. Luke 4:14 is talking about when Jesus returned from being tested in the wilderness, and it says the following, "Jesus returned to Galilee in the power of the Spirit....."

He then also stated in John 14:12, "Very truly I tell you, whoever believes in me will do the works I have been doing, and they will do even greater things than these, because I am going to the Father." This is the part a lot of believers miss. We receive the Holy Spirit within us but fail to recognize that to be all that God called us to be, and to do what He called us to do, we must be baptized in the Holy Spirit. The Scriptures say that Jesus's public ministry began only when He was clothed with power by the Spirit.

So, the Holy Spirit was already dwelling within me because I had given my life to the Lord. But I was not walking in the supernatural ways of the Kingdom because I hadn't experienced the power of God through the Holy Spirit. It's the same Spirit, but two different purposes.

The woman at the retreat came over to me and started praying for me. I couldn't tell you what she prayed or what was spoken, but I vividly remember my mouth starting to open up and form words I had no understanding of. I was hesitant to speak loudly because I had no idea what was coming out of my mouth either. She encouraged me to not hold back, and at once, all these words came rushing from my mouth. Dropping to my knees, I laid on the ground, sobbing, for over half an hour. Nothing in me could stop the words from rushing out, and nothing in me could stop myself from crying. Now, you have to understand that I hated being the one that everyone was looking at.

I cared about what people thought, and this, for sure, didn't look put together or normal. I never let myself be this vulnerable and emotional around people I didn't know, but I wasn't thinking about any of that in this moment.

You might be reading this and wondering why I was crying. Well, I had always known that God loved me and had heard it said a thousand times, but I had no idea what that really meant. In that moment, I experienced the love of Jesus like I had never felt before. It was as if I was getting just a little glimpse of His heart for me for the first time, and I had no other reaction than to cry at feeling the weight of that love. I can't fully explain or do it justice to what I was feeling, but I was so overwhelmed by His love for me. I had no idea that He was that near to me and that I could feel Him in that way so deeply.

I also had no understanding of what speaking in tongues was. I didn't grow up in a Pentecostal church, had never heard anyone speak in tongues before, or a sermon preached on it. I had heard it mentioned maybe a handful of times and seen it said in Acts 2:4, "All of them were filled with the Holy Spirit and began to speak in other tongues as the Spirit enabled them," but that was the extent of my knowledge or experience. Now looking back on the experience, I realize it was actually the wisdom of the Holy Spirit that I knew what it was. I remember thinking, *I have no idea what speaking in tongues is, except that I'm pretty sure this is it.* It wasn't something I had prayed for or even wanted. It was the pursuit of God chasing me down, meeting that heart cry I had been praying of wanting more of Him.

It amazes me to this day that the Lord can meet us right where we are at. Someone who had no grid for any of this, He would still pour out His Spirit on me. How He can see the hunger in someone's life and fill it with what they need. How He can choose us, even the Creator of the Universe, to pour out His Spirit on, even when we don't have any idea what He's doing.

Back to that same retreat: I was prophesied over for the first time in my life and received words from the Lord through His people that would begin the outpouring of words to come over the calling of my life. I would notice the months to come after leaving that retreat, the way that I thought about people and looked at them, was so different. I had a care for people that I didn't have previously. I would pray for people that the Lord showed me and felt love for people I didn't even know. There was compassion I had never felt before, and my heart was breaking for His people.

Before going to that retreat, I was discouraged and feeling hopeless because I didn't really know God, even though I said I did. The things I had gone through in life and the lack of a consistent relationship with Jesus led to never being fully satisfied or hopeful.

I left that retreat feeling empowered, excited, and full of the Holy Spirit. However, I had no idea the journey He was starting to take me on.

Before we go on to the next chapter, I feel that there are some of you reading this who have felt a lot of things I described earlier. You have known that there is more of Jesus, but you have no idea how to get it or what it looks like. If that's you, take a few minutes to invite His presence into the space you are in. Bring your hunger before the Lord and ask Him to fill you. You can pray your own prayer or pray something like this:

Holy Spirit, I thank you that you dwell within me. That when I gave you my life and committed it to you, you made your home inside of me. I thank you for the gift of the Holy Spirit. I know that you want to reveal more of your presence to me. So right now, Lord, I ask that you would baptize me with your Holy Spirit, to do the work of the Father and fill me up with power. In the book of Acts, it says that all were filled with the Holy Spirit. I thank you,

Lord, that I am part of the all, that that is my inheritance as well, and I receive it for myself.

You might feel Him come in the form of heat, with His deep love, crying, speaking in tongues or any other way that He wants to. Don't rush on and let Him come however He sees fit. He is eager to meet with you today. There are some of you reading this that your life will not be the same from this day forward.

Let Him move whatever way He wants to move in you.

THE HOLY LAND

("Our Father": Bethel Music)

So, I just had this insanely beautiful encounter with the Lord at the retreat, and I'm still trying to wrap my head around all of it. From that day forward, I began to have encounters with the Lord that were like nothing else I had experienced beforehand. I was experiencing Him in a measure I didn't know was possible on earth. It became very normal to me to feel the Holy Spirit in me, or resting on me very regularly, usually in the form of deep peace. Around this time, Miski informed me she was going to do a three-week intensive class through our college to Israel. This particular class was a mixture of learning in a classroom setting while in Israel and then taking what you are learning and applying it practically by seeing the sites we are studying about. Basically, this equated to walking an extensive amount of miles a day and eating more pita than I've ever eaten in my life! My mom urged me to sign up to go, but I just didn't have any interest.

On the last day possible, I decided that it could be fun to be in another country with my best friend and decided to apply. No other reason. Not because of the class, not because of the country, but simply because my friend was going. I've since learned that sometimes the best thing you can do is take a leap of faith and just say yes. You never know what might happen, and how God can be orchestrating things together for your good.

I got accepted into the class and at the end of my junior year in 2016, I packed up my bags to head to the Holy Land for three weeks during the summer. I could tell so many beautiful stories of my time there, but I want to highlight one that particularly changed my life going forward.

Everywhere we were going, we were recounting the stories of the healings that Jesus did in those places. Story after story, Jesus touched and healed person after person and then would continue on, walking to the next destination. I knew that Jesus loved me and saw me, but I couldn't help but feel like just another one in the crowd when I recounted these stories. I know it might sound silly, but I started praying that Jesus would show me where He was personally in my life, that I would know He loved me deeply and saw me.

About a week into our trip, my friends and I found out about a worship night being hosted at a church right up the street from our hotel. We had plans that night with other people from the trip but ended up opting out to go to the worship event. I couldn't shake this feeling that I knew I had to be there. We ended up finding out a team from Bethel School of Supernatural Ministry, also a part of Bethel Church in Redding, California, was leading the worship night. Their school was on mission trips the week that we were there. Not that that meant much to me at the time, since I hardly knew anything about them.

Have you ever spent time dreaming about something or imagining how something could be and then it finally happens, and it all just feels like a dream? That's exactly what I felt from this worship night. I can remember we started singing the song mentioned next to this chapter's title, "Our Father," at some point in the night. The worship leaders who were leading the song had us turn to each corner of the room, each direction (north, east, south, and west) and declare, "Let heaven come," one of the main parts of the song.

The sound in the place erupted as people cried out and sang with everything inside of them that heaven would be made manifest on earth. It wasn't just a nice, little thing to say; I realized these people truly believed it and were praying and singing with a boldness I hadn't seen before. There was something different about this worship, as I could feel the tangible presence of God in this place. These were not people who attended church on Sundays and carried on with the rest of their lives until the next weekend. These people centered their lives around Jesus, and it was so evident in the way they worshipped. Everything inside me came alive this night. This was similar to how I had worshipped for so long on my own but had never seen a room full of people worship the same way.

After worship, some of the students from the school called out sicknesses and physical problems that the Lord had shown them people were battling in the crowd, and people were healed that night right there! I had never seen anything like that in my life, but I knew I wanted to see more. I always had believed God was the Healer, but I didn't realize He still healed in that way through His people to this day.

At the end of the night, everyone continued worshipping and opened up the room for anyone to come up to the front to get prayer from the team. This had happened one other time in my life, but the room became extremely blurry during this call; it was as if I saw a direct line to one person in the room. I made a beeline for this older man on the prayer team and asked him to pray for me. He asked if there was anything in particular, and I said no. He then prayed for me, and for the life of me, I couldn't tell you what he prayed over me that night.

What I can tell you is what he said to me, once he was done praying, because it is forever engrained in my memory and is the first time I ever felt deeply known by the Lord. He looked at me and told me Jesus loves me. I replied, with a smile, "I know, thank you." He then looked at me again, directly in my eyes, and said, "No, Jesus really loves you. You need to know how much He loves you and that He sees you." He began to tell me how much I was seen and known by Jesus, confirming everything I had asked the Lord to show me.

I walked away and fell to the floor sobbing as the worship continued. If I'm being honest with you, I didn't expect that prayer to be answered, and I didn't expect it to be answered so quickly. At this point in my life, I knew that Jesus showed up for the major things in life and when He wanted to, but I didn't know He would go to lengthy measures to respond to my voice, to hear me, and to speak to me. I didn't know He was that involved in my life and would move heaven and earth to speak to me and meet with me. Something shifted within my heart that night, as if a part of me broke open, a part I didn't know needed to be loved so deeply. A purpose bigger than myself started to emerge, and walls I had held up began to slowly crumble.

God would later speak to me in depth about that night. "Let heaven come" was my inheritance, my calling, and my prayer.

Let heaven come is YOUR inheritance, YOUR call, and YOUR prayer.

What does that mean?

Colossians 3:1: "Since, then, you have been raised with Christ, set your hearts on things above, where Christ is, seated at the right hand of God." (NIV) The New Living Translation puts it this way, "Set your sights on the realities of heaven."

Matthew 16:19: "I will give you the keys of the kingdom of heaven; whatever you bind on earth will be bound in heaven, and whatever you loose on earth will be loosed in heaven."

Your inheritance is your heavenly seat. Yes, it's your eternal salvation, but so often we just stop there. The abovementioned verse in Colossians shows us that we were raised with Christ; therefore, we should set our sights on "the realities of heaven" because that is our standard to live by. And then in the verse in Matthew, Jesus Himself tells us that the keys of heaven are ours. What does that mean? That means as children of God, we have full access to the throne room. We have full access to the Kingdom of God. We have full access to the King, and whatever is in heaven is made to inhabit the earth.

Matthew 11:12 says, "From the days of John the Baptist until now, the kingdom of heaven has been subjected to violence, and violent people have been raiding it." The word "violence/violent" in the initial Greek is actually the word for "by force," meaning that people are taking the kingdom by force. In other words, the kingdom of heaven is not something you lightly pull on. You take it by force, meaning it is the lifeline in which you breathe, operate, and live from. Your inheritance as a son or daughter of Christ is to let heaven come to earth.

Matthew 28:18-20 says, "Then Jesus came to them and said, "All authority in heaven and on earth has been given to me. Therefore go and make disciples of all nations, baptizing them in the name of the Father and pf the Son and of the Holy Spirit, and teaching them to obey everything I have commanded you. And surely, I am with you always, to the very end of the age.'"

This statement Jesus made is a commissioning statement, as He first tells us of our inheritance. He says that all authority in heaven and on earth is His. And then from that place, He gives a commissioning statement to step out in faith. He gives us a call, reminding us of who He is, the God we serve, and then says, from that place, that we have the same access to bring heaven to earth because of who our Father is.

That line, "let heaven come," would constantly bring me back to another call that Jesus gave in John 14:12: "Very truly I tell you, whoever believes in me will do the works I have been doing, and they will do even greater things than these, because I am going to the Father." We won't see heaven in all its fullness until Jesus returns, but we are called to let God invade our world with the realities of heaven, saturating it with His presence as people encounter His love, healing, miracles, signs, and wonders.

This is our purpose on this earth to see Jesus get honor and glory through simply sharing about the love we have encountered through Him. We aren't getting a full representation of the Father if we don't have the power of God at work in our lives. So often, believers aren't walking in the truth of the power that lives inside of them, which is there because of who lives in us. Heaven is a person; His name is Jesus, and we're called to let heaven come everywhere we go, being obedient to what Jesus is doing and saying. "Let heaven come" is our calling.

Psalm 2:8: "Ask me, and I will make the nations your inheritance, the ends of the earth your possession."

Matthew 6:9-10: "This, then, is how you should pray: 'Our Father in heaven, hallowed be your name, your kingdom come, your will be done, on earth as it is in heaven.'"

The last verse shows us how to pray. That we pray for the will of God to be done on earth, that we pray the veil between heaven and earth would be so non-existent because of the manifested presence of heaven on earth. "Let heaven come" is our prayer.

Little did I know that in just over a year, I would pack up my whole life and move cross country to attend Bethel School of Supernatural Ministry, the school of the team that was in Israel during my trip. I had absolutely no clue what I was doing with my life after college at that point, but I was about to start one of the wildest years of my life in a little over a year.

My whole life was soon going to be radically altered. But I'm getting ahead of myself. Let's go to senior year of college...

BEAN BAG

("Reckless Love": Cory Asbury)

SENIOR YEAR OF COLLEGE STARTED THE COFFEE ADDICTION, FOR sure, for me! If there's one addiction I've had that I'm completely okay not being set free from, that's coffee! If you know me, you know that nine out of ten times, I will be holding a cup of coffee in my hand.

I ended up living in San Francisco for a semester, doing an internship there as part of my social work degree. I had no idea how much coffee was a normal part of people's lives there and was about to be a part of mine as well. It definitely didn't help that all the coffee places were so cute!

There was this one particular spot right down the street from where I lived that I would visit at least twice a week. It wasn't the cutest place, or had the best coffee in the city, but it became my place. Looking back at it, I think it became my place because that's where I really found my independence. Well not exactly from the coffee shop, but in San Francisco. I would venture often to this little café called Bean Bag just to journal and write. I had a lot of good cups of coffee there with friends, sweet morning breakfasts, and conversations with Jesus that really shaped my life. It was the place I decided to officially apply to Bethel, so I think in some way that little coffee place on Divisadero Street will always resonate with me as having a big part in my story.

I always would find it funny when people, mostly conservative Christians, would say to me, "Wow, you're in a really liberal place. I couldn't live there." Or they would talk about it as if it was a place that was far gone, saying it must be hard to be a Christian there. Have we forgotten that the Jesus we serve is the light in the middle of darkness? That the early disciples thrived in persecution and trouble? That our God is so much bigger than any city we are in? That we are called to be the light that changes the cities we inhabit? Just a few thoughts...

I actually deepened my relationship with Jesus during my time in San Francisco more than I ever had at any other time in my life. I started really reading my Bible consistently for the first time and praying. I really started seeking my faith for myself and evaluating my life, what I wanted and what was important to me.

At this point, I knew that I had one semester left, which was before graduation. I thought about the possibility of going to grad school, but after praying about it, it just didn't feel like that was what I was supposed to do. I started getting the idea that maybe I should attend some kind of a ministry school, so I wrote down a bunch of schools and programs and started researching all of them extensively. Bethel was on the list but was the very last one, being the most out of my comfort zone, so naturally I put it on the bottom. I should've known just from that reaction that the Lord was going to send me there!

I want to share this part of the story with you, and how I ended up saying yes, because the hand of God was so clearly on my life to get me there; and it's one of my favorite stories! So, I mentioned that I was doing an internship while in San Francisco. Well, long story short, I was volunteering one night at one of the community events my organization, City Hope, was hosting and ended up connecting with a young woman who was also volunteering there.

We hit it off and started to grab coffee and get together frequently. At this point, no one really knew about the possibility of me going to Bethel. To be honest with you, the only time I had heard of Bethel, besides a few of their worship songs and the time the team was there in Israel, was when my roommate Miski had mentioned years prior that she wanted to go there someday. In my head at the time, all I was thinking was, *Make a mental note, Allecia, to never go there*, because it sounded like nothing I wanted to be a part of. Ha! Little did I know…

As I continued to look into different ministry schools and Bible colleges, I began to cross each one off the list. There was no peace with any of them, and soon enough, the only one that remained on my list was Bethel. So, I started researching it and praying about the possibility of going there.

It was one of the last weeks I had left in San Francisco before coming back home to the East Coast to finish up the second semester of my senior year. My friend, the one I had met volunteering, and I went to Bean Bag to grab coffee together one last time. It was there that I shared with her I was interested in attending this ministry school called Bethel. She looked at me taken aback and went on to explain to me an interaction that would solidify my plans to attend Bethel.

Just days prior, she had gone to the grocery store. She was telling her cashier that she had just come from church, and he started asking her what church she went to in the city. He ended up telling her that he was now living in town but had just moved from Redding, California, where he attended Bethel Church and school. My friend and the cashier exchanged numbers because she was interested in hearing more about his experience there. So, when I mentioned Bethel to her, she immediately connected me with the guy to have a conversation.

I left San Francisco shortly after and ended up not having a conversation with the guy until I arrived home to Connecticut. The conversation lasted two hours as he shared with me all about his experience there. He shared about encounters and moments that shaped his life while he was there, and the hunger of the people at the school to just want to know Jesus more. As soon as I hung up the phone, I applied to Bethel. I knew that this was exactly where I needed to be and was so beyond excited.

I watched in awe as things began to fall into place, and I was amazed at how God took care of all the details for going to Bethel. The school had told me they would notify me with a decision in two weeks, which kinda bummed me out because my family was coming up that weekend to visit me at school in Massachusetts, and I wanted to tell them in person if I got accepted. Jesus then told me the exact day I would find out that I was accepted, the day before my family was to get there. Sure enough, I find out I was accepted the day He told me I was, and I was able to tell my family in person. I was starting to see how much Jesus really was in all the details.

Next came the five-hundred-dollar deposit that I had to pay for the school. Now you have to know that at this time, once I got accepted, I was fully prepared to move across the country to Redding. I didn't know anyone or anything, and to be quite honest, I probably had enough money to last me for four months at best.

So, it came time to put down my deposit, and I was feeling the weight of the decision. It was a nice thing to say I trusted Jesus, but once I put down five hundred dollars, I wouldn't get that back. That meant then I would need to pay off the rest of my tuition, which was still two thousand dollars, and have money for an apartment, food, gas, etc., to last me for the nine months of the program.

Once I put down that deposit, it was representing my faith in action. I couldn't just say I trusted Jesus, while having a backup plan in mind. He either needed to come through like He said He would, or I was screwed. I hesitated putting that money down until the last possible second because I wasn't feeling complete peace. I realized I didn't have peace because I didn't actually know if I trusted Jesus to come through for me in this way. And then on the last night to send in my deadline, I knew He was asking me to just choose to trust Him.

Sometimes I think we're waiting on the feeling of trust. We're waiting to say, "I feel like I can trust you." And what I've figured out is that sometimes, we need to choose to trust. I recalled every way in which I was able to trust Him before, as it felt safer to me to be able to see the full outcome and then to say yes to trusting Him. But I couldn't see the outcome; I couldn't see if all the money would come through; I couldn't see if I would fall flat on my face trying to move across the country, but He wasn't asking me to see the full picture. Faith is seeing only the steps in front of you and choosing to step forward. Hebrews 11:1 says, "Now faith is confidence in what we hope for and assurance about what we do not see." So, I said, "Ok, I'm gonna put this money down. And I've never seen you come through for me in finances like this, but because I've been able to trust you before, I'll trust you now." I sent my five hundred dollars through, which depleted me of a large portion of the money I currently had. However, I was left in awe that the second I chose to send it in, the second I chose to step out in faith, I was filled with immense peace.

I instantly knew I was going to be ok. I had no idea how, but I knew Jesus would provide for me like He promised.

So, I finished up my senior year and did a seventeen-day road trip with my family out to California in August of 2017. They drove with me out there so that I would have my car on the other side of the country.

As I packed up my bags and fit it all into my Nissan Sentra, I couldn't help but feel that I was establishing roots deeper than deep. That a foundation of trust was being rooted really deep inside me. I wrote this in my journal in Arizona on the way to California.

When trust is tested … it either crumbles or prevails. When it's stretched beyond its limit, it has the capacity to deteriorate, or it can stand tall like a mountain, unmovable and unshakeable. What is your foundation grounded in? What is your trust built upon? Faith is the mountain that sustains, the rock that can't be moved, because the foundation is rooted in truth.

I think us Christians can get really good at saying things about Jesus that we know to be truth, but we leave no room for Him to show up in that area of our lives. It becomes a theory we talk about rather than an experience we live and learn from.

There are two outcomes when you choose to trust in something. Either it crumbles or prevails, based on what you are putting your trust in. I've heard the saying a lot that God will never give you more than you can handle, but I would wildly disagree with that thought. I think it's a nice, little sentence that makes us feel safe, and might make for a good bumper sticker, but requires no faith. It doesn't require choosing to step out of our comfort zones. I believe Jesus calls us into adventures time and time again, giving us the choice to come along and say yes. He already prepared the trip and knows every corner and turn. And If I've learned one thing from those adventures, it is that true God adventures could never have been fulfilled on your own. He will only call you into something that requires more dependency on Him, more leaning on Him. If I were to step into something that I can complete on my own, my dream is too small. But when it's His dream, and His adventure, there isn't a chance in hell I could do it without Him.

So, when we choose to trust Him in something, we leave room for our roots to dig down deep in faith. Our foundation of our faith continues to grow as we continue to trust, time and time again. We establish something bigger than ourselves as we say yes to God. When our faith is built on shaky ground, it's only a matter of time before something crumbles our faith. But when we choose to trust Jesus, I promise you those roots will be watered and only grow deeper and deeper.

What do you need to trust Him with today? What can you give Him, saying, "I might not trust you fully with this, but I'm going to choose to trust you and see it through with you"? Be specific. Let Him show you that He can be trusted with the deepest parts of your heart, whether it's with finances, a job, your family, a spouse, a friendship, your health, etc.

And if you're having a hard time with the idea of trusting Jesus, remember that He can be trusted because He gives without requirement. He died a death for you and I that cost Him every-thing, knowing that some people would never choose Him back. Only a love void of all pride and selfishness can commit an act of sacrifice like that. Only a love that tore through hell to find you and capture your heart can do something that costly. His trust isn't like the broken trust that you might've seen time and time again. His promises are true, and He is good and faithful to His Word. Deuteronomy 7:9 says, "Know therefore that the Lord your God is God; he is the faithful God, keeping his covenant of love to a thousand generations of those who love him and keep his commandments."

If nothing else up until this point, I hope you've seen the ways Jesus came after my heart for years. That He moves with action toward His kids, and He moves with action toward you.

Start recalling the times where Jesus was there, the ways in which He pursued you even when you were lost and broken and far away from Him. The intimate moments that only you and Him know of, where He captivated you and showed up in a way that was so specific to you. The moments He sent someone else to encourage you and share Jesus with you.

Some of you can't think of any memories like that, and that's ok. I promise you He was still pursuing you in those times. Ask Him right now to start showing you where He was when you were crying alone in your bed, when you were enjoying celebrating your birthday, when you felt alone and scared, when you accomplished something great.

Remember that He's in the details, and if you start asking Him, He will show you the way.

Remember that He loves revealing His heart for you. He loves to reveal how He's pursued you. By nature, that's who He is. He is a pursuer.

He doesn't require us to pursue Him back, but He wants us to because our hearts are so important to Him.

I could easily write a whole book on the next three years of my life at Bethel, but I want to share specific encounters, testimonies, and things I learned along the way that I feel are crucial for this book. My hope is that as you continue reading, you would see the pursuit of God's heart after mine, and that you would also see what it begins to look like when one of His kids reflects on what He's doing and pursues Him back with everything inside of her.

My hope is that you would so clearly see the pursuit of the Father after your own heart, and that you would be ignited with a fresh fire to pursue Him wholeheartedly.

one.

WHO AM I?

("You Say": Lauren Daigle and "Who You Say I Am": Hillsong)

WHAT DO YOU SEE WHEN YOU LOOK IN THE MIRROR? DO YOU SEE someone you love being? Do you see bravery, regret, happiness, sadness, confidence, insecurity? Do you see someone who has overcome a lot or someone who has been weighed down by life? Do you see a person you're really proud of, or do you wonder how you've gotten to be so far away from who you thought you'd be?

Maybe, like me, you realized you were looking in the mirror from the wrong perspective. That who was looking back at you was someone so much better than you imagined, but you had been too stuck reflecting on who they weren't. Did you know that God likes to focus more on who you are than who you aren't? I know, this one messed me up too.

I tend to be a perfectionist, thinking a lot about the things that I do and say and hold myself to a really high standard. I put a lot of unnecessary pressure on myself (still working on this one) and think a lot more of us tend to put pressure on ourselves than we care to admit. I found that most of my thoughts about myself weren't super kind or positive, and I tended to dwell way more on what I did wrong or could've done better than what I did right.

We did this one exercise called "mirror ministry" at Bethel one day, where someone basically leads you through inner healing while you're looking into a mirror. I watched myself as I struggled to make eye contact with my own eyes in the mirror. Tears welled up as I fought off the desire to look away. It was then that I realized my self-worth still needed some drastic work.

I think when a lot of people hear that I went to ministry school, they tend to think that all I did was sit in a classroom all day and read the Bible. That's like twenty percent truth. Anyone who attended Bethel would tell you that it's more like heart surgery than anything else. It's really tough and can be really painful, but it is also so, so rewarding. You might say, "Well, how did you have that much to work on and through?" Well, I realized I truly didn't know myself, and I had A LOT to learn about Jesus. I had spent years of my life trying to figure out my identity apart from Him, which is impossible. No one can truly know who they were fully created to be outside of the One who created them. So, I needed to go back to the One who created me, who formed me, and who knew me deeply.

And there was also something the Lord showed me that gave me a whole new perspective. One day, I was spending time worshipping Him and was telling Him that He was so holy, that He was so righteous, that He was so beautiful.

I started singing a song by Hillsong about us being who He says we are. But as I started to sing those lyrics, a song that I've sung a hundred times, the lyrics changed as they came out of my mouth. It turned into, "I am who I say you are." I sat there baffled by this statement as tears poured over the brim of my eyes, because I was having a revelation of the way Jesus sees us. The way we view ourselves isn't how He views us. The tears poured over as He began to tell me who I was, reciting everything back to me that I just said He was. He said, "You are holy. You are righteous. You are beautiful." Everything I said about Him, He mirrored back to me.

You are a reflection of Him. Since you were made in His image, you were created with the nature of God. You are holy because He is holy. You are righteous because He is righteous. You are beautiful because He created you and says you are. We can no longer separate our identity from His. We can no longer try to find our identity outside of Him.

Psalm 139:17-18 says this, "How precious to me are your thoughts, God! How vast is the sum of them! Were I to count them, they would outnumber the grains of sand—when I awake, I am still with you."

If His thoughts are that numerous about us, we should probably spend more time finding out what He says about us, letting that change the way we live and see ourselves.

So, I started the journey of healing with Him, letting Him replace all the lies I had believed about Him and myself. Author Blake Healy talks about how our belief in God's intent toward us creates a standard that shapes the way we see the world and, ultimately, the way we see Him.

Who is God to you?

Is He an angry God?

Is He a loving Father?

Do you view Him as being disappointed in you?

Is He full of compassion and proud of you?

Is He a far-off idea, or is He near?

Is He distant, or is He a dad to you?

We create a lens in which we see the world by the way we've answered these questions. Let God redefine these answers for you. And let me give you a little tip: Everyone lately seems to be searching for their truth, who they are, and how to attain and maintain it.

Soul-searching is good, but it will only get you so far. Apart from Jesus, we cannot know our full selves. And it's a lifelong journey toward discovery. Soul-searching doesn't bring a simple answer, a perfect boxed label. As we are constantly finding out more of who God is, we find out more of who we are. But take it from me, it's way easier to search His heart for us first. I tried figuring out who I was and then who He was, but apart from Him, I could only get so far in my journey. As you continue to seek His heart, you can't help but find out more of who you are, hidden in the depths of Him.

THE VOICE IN THE NOISE

("Voice of God": Dante Bowe)

I grew up hearing Jesus's voice ever since I was little. It wasn't often, but it also wasn't unusual for me to know He was speaking to me. As I grew up and grew more in my relationship with Him, I started to see how clearly I heard Him. I would question His voice a lot in the beginning, thinking maybe I couldn't hear Him as clearly as I did, but the more time I got alone with God, the more I learned to recognize His voice in the middle of the noise. If you can't hear His voice in the stillness, you won't hear Him amid the chaos.

It was my first weekend in Redding, with Bethel, and I had heard of a worship night happening that I decided to attend. I hopped in my car and drove to this house at the end of a dirt road and made my way inside. The house was jam-packed; you couldn't move without bumping into someone else. There were easily over two hundred people crammed inside this little house. We socialized and introduced and re-introduced ourselves as we tried to remember the people's names we just met and what country they were from. And then the worship started, carrying on late into the night as people kept gathering in and spilled out onto the porch. All the windows and doors were open, and it was clear that these people were here for one thing: Jesus. I marveled at people who had come from all over the world and were all singing the same name inside this house on the dirt road in Northern California. Each person had a story of how they got there, of how God uniquely called each individual there to this little town in the middle of nowhere California.

It was a little over a hundred degrees outside, but that didn't stop people from shouting and dancing and singing with everything they had inside of them. It wasn't just hype; you could actually tangibly feel faith in the room. That these people were being moved to their core by pure faith, love, and affection for Jesus. I sat there shocked that there were people who loved Jesus this much, who laid their whole lives down to come to this place because He asked them too. There was no breeze that night in the air; it was hot and dry, but every once in a while, throughout the night, we would feel this rush of air fill the room, a wind blowing through the house. There was no movement of anything else with this breeze, no trees outside wailing about, but this wind felt different, supernatural if you will. I knew I was beginning to see a taste of heaven made manifest on earth.

I was fascinated by the nearness of Jesus, that He was this close to me all the time and that I could feel His nearness. So, I leaned into that newfound reality and started talking to Him more, seeing how much He would converse back with me. There was one day in particular where I was planning on taking a trip to San Francisco with my friend who was visiting. I quite honestly didn't have money to go, and I can remember praying a prayer that I thought was silly at the time. I said, "Jesus, I just need fifty dollars; that would be super helpful." I wasn't being very serious when I prayed this request; it was more of just one of those prayers ya throw up and hope that maybe something will happen, and, by some chance, a blessing will rain down.

So, I went with my friend to San Francisco for the weekend, hoping that this wouldn't screw me over later on financially. We sat on the bus one night, headed to dinner, when I got a phone call from my college roommate. I started to share with her everything God was doing in my life at Bethel so far, and then it came time to get off at our stop. I stood up and walked toward the door to exit when I felt a hand tap me on my shoulder. Turning around, I saw an older man who smiled at me and slipped cash into my hand, telling me to use it to buy something.

I walked out of the bus in shock at what had just happened. Forgetting that the money was still clutched in my hand for a second, I opened my palm to see a fifty-dollar bill lying in it. My tears filled to the brim (those past three years had really brought out the emotional side I had suppressed for years), as I was reminded yet again that every prayer is heard, and every need is met, by the Lord.

I decided to ask Jesus later on what to do with the money, and I heard Him say to give it away. I sat there confused, not sure why He would give me something to then only ask to depart from it and not even use it on myself. But I agreed. I then asked who I should give it to, and He told me I would know who and when it was time. Now, you might be wondering how I knew I was hearing from God so clearly. But truth be told, at this point I wasn't sure. I was pretty sure I heard Him speaking these things to me, but I realized that the only way to know for sure was to listen and see if what I thought I had heard came to pass.

Fast forward a little over a month later, I was in my revival group (a group made up of seventy students that met weekly) where they decided to take up an offering for some people within the group. I knew immediately that I was supposed to give the money. I asked the Lord who He wanted it to go to, and He showed me one of the men in our group that we were taking up an offering for. I can remember feeling I didn't want to give the money away; it was mine after all, wasn't it? And was I being foolish giving away money that I needed for myself? Instantly, I felt the Lord telling me that it wasn't my money to begin with, and pride and fear started breaking off me. I handed the money over, full of joy at that point, to the man, hearing the Lord say to me, "I will double it in your life."

Double what? Double the money? That made no sense to me, but I was starting to see the Lord did a lot of things that didn't make sense to me. I said, "Ok, if you say you will, you will. I guess we'll see."

About a week later, the man who I had given the money to reached out to me, asking if I still had tuition money left that needed to be paid. I answered yes, and he explained that someone had given him money recently, and he felt like he was supposed to bless me with it and pay toward my tuition. Do you know how much it was? That's right, you better believe it was one hundred dollars! It was exactly doubled. I was so blown away by the faithfulness of Jesus.

I can share story after story of God doing things like this hundreds of times in the last few years in my life, and every time they are unique and never fail to leave me in wonder all over again of who He is.

But in the middle of all those stories, I learned a very important lesson. Sometimes the blessings pour down in abundance, and other times, it requires tugging on the robe of the One who sits in heaven. Sometimes it's about pulling down; other times, it's about reaching within and pulling out. I wonder how many things we aren't seeing because we haven't asked the Lord.

I often wonder if I never asked, even halfheartedly, to see God show up in the small detail of the fifty dollars, if I would've seen it. And if I hadn't asked Him what to do with the money, if that man in my group would've been blessed with it, and if I would've received a double portion of what I asked for. It amazes me that behind my simple asking, there was a blessing waiting for someone else and a bigger blessing than I expected waiting in return for me. Jesus always does above and beyond with the simple "yes" we give Him.

What blessings are waiting for you because you simply haven't asked?

On the way to go and see Jairus's daughter, who was dying, Jesus stopped and talked to the woman who pulled on the hem of his cloak. "Daughter, your faith has healed you. Go in peace and be freed from your suffering," Jesus exclaimed in Mark 5:34, as news was reported back that Jairus's daughter had officially died. She died in the process of Him bringing freedom and life to another. However, Jesus wasn't worried. He wasn't anxiously running but simply carried on down the road and, upon arriving at the house, grabbed her hand and said, "Talitha koum" (Little girl, I say to you, get up). He has extended an invitation for you to pull on the hem of His cloak. This is where the lines between heaven and earth become blurred. Where we reach out, saying, "If I just pull on the hem of His cloak.….."

We can easily look at this story and see Jairus's daughter as being the one who was in need of an answer critically, rather than the woman who pulled on the hem of Jesus's cloak. One woman had died, and another one had had a condition of constant bleeding for twelve years straight. Yet He answered her prayer in the middle of answering another one. One is not partial to the other; one is not more important than the other. They were both equally important in the eyes of Jesus because the Father loved them both.

Your prayers and requests, no matter how big or small, are all important to God. He once spoke this to me, saying, "I concern myself with the matters of your heart." In other words, He cares about what you care about.

Just like a good dad, God might say no, but that's only because He has even better plans for you than what you planned. And, just like a child, we can come freely and ask openly of Him. It's our joy and right to ask, and He reveals the answer to us in the waiting.

What are some things you've been hesitant to ask Him for because you've been scared He won't come through for you?

I was terrified that He wouldn't come through like the provider I was told He was. My first year of ministry school, the Lord asked me not to get a job. This didn't make sense to a lot of people outside of the environment that I was in, but I knew He was building my trust in Him in this area. It gave me the space I needed in that season to strengthen my relationship with Him and prioritize my healing.

What's an area you are having a hard time trusting Him in? If there's an area that is coming to mind for you, ask Him how you can partner with Him to put yourself out of your comfort zone and watch Him come through for you. When we give Him room and put our own agendas and comforts aside, I promise you He always comes and meets you.

It was through constantly letting Him show up in my life, and listening to the small nudging of what I thought was His voice, that I learned how to hear Him more clearly, no matter if it was in the stillness or in the chaos.

May I suggest to you to remember that He is always speaking. Some seasons He might be quieter than others, but I wouldn't necessarily say that He's silent. I would say more times than not, He's speaking in a new way. He speaks in dreams, through His written Word in the Bible, prophetic words given, a sermon, through a friend, a thought or nudging in your spirit, etc. But just like the song I mentioned in the beginning of this chapter says, His voice can be found in everything and everywhere. Take a moment to listen to the song above called "Voice of God," and then I would encourage you to pick a way in which you want to see Him this week and ask Him to show up for you in that way.

He might show up just in the way you asked Him to, or He might surprise you and show up in an entirely different way. But either way, remember the main thing is that He came when you asked Him to. The goal is to always have more of Him, no matter what it looks like. He is the goal. He is the main reward. Not the things He can do for us, but the person of Jesus Himself.

THE VEIL WAS THIN IN
MEXICO

("Too Good To Not Believe": Brandon Lake)

"AND WHEN JESUS HAD CRIED OUT AGAIN IN A LOUD VOICE, HE gave up his spirit. At that moment, the curtain of the temple was torn in two from top to bottom." (Matthew 27:50-51)

The splitting of the veil, through Jesus's sacrifice, was the splitting of distance between you and the Father. What I mean by that is this. Prior to this, you would have to go to the Temple to meet with God; that was where He dwelled. But when the veil was torn, heaven was now so much closer to us. God now made His home inside anyone who believed in Him. You didn't need to go to the Temple to meet with Him. You could meet with Him whenever you wanted. It was the solidifying of what Jesus was teaching, preaching, and showing people here on earth.

The word here "torn" is the same word in the original Hebrew language in Mark 1:10: "Just as Jesus was coming up out of the water, he saw heaven being torn open and the Spirit descending on Him like a dove."

The word torn is an aggressive word in nature, meaning to rip apart, which is not a tender act. The veil was violently torn, and the heavens were violently torn open. It's an act full of love and mercy. It was God's way of saying, "I am coming to pour out Myself on My children." It's an unthinkable act of love. When the heavens were torn open, and the Spirit descended upon Jesus, He would then go into the wilderness and come out clothed with power, where the Holy Spirit flowed from Him in a constant outpouring. The tearing of the heavens was a tearing of a spiritual veil, where heaven and earth weren't separate but, rather, the lines became quite blurry in the ways Jesus would start bringing heaven to earth through His spirit and through His people. In the same way when the veil was torn in two, the resurrected Jesus would now dwell within us in a constant outpouring of His presence. He operated and lived from being under an open heaven, having direct access to God, and we are to do the same.

I had been learning a lot about this truth from being at Bethel. Specifically, learning what this means practically as Christians and how we get to live and walk that out in our daily lives. But I don't think it was until I went to Mexico that year on a mission trip that I saw more fully what Jesus had in mind.

Something felt different as soon as my feet hit the ground in Mexico. I was there on a mission's trip, partnering with local churches and communities to share Jesus with the Mexican people and serve them however they needed us to. It's almost like I could feel it in the air when we got there; there was a level of faith there that I knew God was going to move powerfully.

I soon would learn that most of the Mexican people believed in God. Now, their idea of God was more based on religious duties than having an intimate, personal relationship with Him, but nonetheless, almost everyone you talked to believed in God. It was a lot different than in the States, where you wouldn't assume everyone you talked to believed in Him.

I had asked the Lord to give me very specific prophetic words for people when we were there, and He did. And to be honest with you, I hadn't experienced Him speaking like that so vividly before in that way to me about other people. There was one day we went to a church leader meeting, and our team called out words of knowledge that Jesus had given us about different health conditions and physical ailments in the room. I felt like Jesus had told me that there was someone there at that meeting with knee pain. Now, typically, I wouldn't have inquired further about that knowledge, but I asked the Lord to give me more specifics related to what I felt like I had heard.

I then heard Him say, "Left knee pain." To me, that felt really risky because I wasn't exactly sure if I was hearing Him one hundred percent correctly or not. But as I called it out on the microphone, I witnessed the pastor of one of the local churches raise his hand, confirming it was him who had the left knee pain. We watched as the Lord radically healed him as we prayed over him! Another man we got to pray over, who also had left knee pain, was healed in an instant, saying he felt heat rushing all throughout his knee and clearing out all pain. I was so overwhelmed that God would give such specifics so that He can heal His kids.

Over and over again, I would witness person after person be healed of physical pain. About ninety-five percent of everyone prayed for in Mexico was healed from pain, which was something I had never before witnessed in my life. I also witnessed a young girl, about fourteen years old, be baptized in the Holy Spirit, as she sobbed under the presence of Jesus's love encountering her. She later ran out of the building to tell people about Jesus. I watched the Mexican people break down crying as they encountered Jesus through prophetic sessions that we did with them.

That moment is so clearly engrained in my mind. I sat with a translator and a local Mexican woman/man as we were given ten to fifteen minutes to prophecy over them and share with them what we felt God was saying over their lives. I watched in wonder, having no strength of my own, as I carried on for two hours, speaking to over twenty people throughout our time there that day. I was in awe because I, myself, had nothing to say to them; I was tired and had never done anything like this before. These beautiful people wanted a word from God, and I had nothing profound to say to them, but as I leaned into the Lord, I saw how much He wanted to speak to His kids. I watched, time and time again, as I continued to rely on Him to touch them.

Words would flow out of my mouth that hit their hearts deeply because it was things I would've never known about them, but only Jesus Himself knew. I would watch women sit in front of me crying as I would share specific things God was sharing with me about them. There's a beauty in watching someone cry, not over something you said they already knew, but in the fact that what you shared couldn't possibly have been known on your own, made them feel seen and known by the Creator of the Universe. I was in awe all over again at how much my simple yes allowed Jesus to crash into the situation radically and meet with His children in fresh, personal ways.

We witnessed people in the trash dumps of Mexico (they lived amongst the trash) be healed, set free, and give their lives to Jesus. I'll never forget one time as my team and I began to worship on top of the mountain that day. The literal trash within the dump started to rise up and encircle us. Without any wind present that day, the trash started rising from the ground and encircled us, twirling upwards in a spiraling circle moving toward the sun. It moved in sync, in the same formation as a tornado, but there was a calmness about the way it moved. It moved steadily, slowly, and somehow followed the piece of trash in front of it. Everyone stopped and stared, and the people living in the dump looked up in wonder, as they began to laugh with joy. They exclaimed they had never seen something like that! To this day, I have never witnessed a more breathtaking moment that I truly believe was God supernaturally moving, reminding us that He gives beauty to ashes, life to decay, and joy for mourning, even in the thick of the mess and debris.

One night, a group of about fifteen of us on the team visited a rehab center. When you entered the center, there was a room full of men and this weird cage-looking thing off to the right, which we learned is where the men went who were rowdier and couldn't be contained as easily. We were there to teach them about Jesus and share stories with them. We were also asked to share stories of healings that we had seen take place earlier that week, so I decided to share my story of the two men healed from left knee pain.

I can remember walking up to the front of the room and being really nervous to speak. All I could think was that there were these men in here who had committed crimes and were a lot tougher than I was. What I had to say wasn't going to soften their hearts or make them want to know Jesus, I believed. However, I tried pushing that thought out of my mind as I approached the front and shared the story of healing with the group. As soon as I finished, I heard the Lord tell me to ask if there was anyone who had been having really bad nightmares in the middle of the night.

I thought, *Oh great, I'm going to ask these tough men to be vulnerable and share if they were having night terrors. This will go over great.* I braced myself as a room full of eyes stared back at me as I asked the question and watched in awe as a man in the front row stood up. He stood up slowly and broke down sobbing, as he shared he had been having horrible night terrors. As I began to pray over him and break those strongholds off him, another man on my team surrounded him and gave him a father's blessing because the Lord had showed him that this young man never had a father figure. This young man crumbled over as he embraced this older man, and I saw that the love of God was running hard after this young man. Countless others were healed, multiple men in the cages were delivered from demons that night, but I couldn't get the image of the young man out of my mind. The man who had no father, who had messed up badly in life, yet still the love of God had been chasing Him down. I was so undone that the Lord would give a specific word to be released that night that He knew His son needed and was so grateful the Lord trusted me to be a part of it.

The thing is, when you see things like this, you're ruined for anything normal. The true person of Jesus will wreck your idea of normal and turn it upside down, because He operates from the lens of the Kingdom of Heaven. And when He extends an invitation to you, you have a choice to step in and see where it takes you, or you can back out, denying what you've seen and heard. The first will cost you more than you ever knew possible and will push you farther out of your comfort zone than you ever wanted to go. But the latter, I've found, will cost you way more, costing you the beauty of living under an open heaven for the cheap lie that preserving dignity and reputation is worth more. In the end, I reasoned that if Jesus died for me to live under an open heaven, I never wanted anything else. I had seen the more of Jesus, and there was no turning back.

The disciples had that choice as well.

Jesus had just finished telling His followers that He was the Bread of Life. In John 6:53, Jesus said the following, "Very truly I tell you, unless you eat the flesh of the Son of Man and drink his blood, you have no life in you." He continued on, and many people walked away from His words because they were offensive to them. And then Jesus turned to the twelve and says to them, recorded in John 6:67, "You do not want to leave too, do you?"

Simon Peter answered Him, "Lord, to whom shall we go? You have the words of eternal life. We have come to believe and to know that you are the Holy One of God" (John 6:68-69).

We look at these verses now and know that Jesus is referencing communion. He's telling us about eternal life, but at the time, these were some crazy sentences He stated. People didn't understand what He was saying, and it was very offensive to them, so they simply walked away.

Now keep in mind, these were people who walked away that had been following Him. They had seen the miracles, signs, and wonders, seen healings and people be set free. Yet, this teaching was too much for them, and they decided to walk away because they didn't understand Jesus's words. They forsook all they saw and knew simply because they couldn't understand.

But Simon Peter's response grips my heart every time. He also doesn't understand and, even in the moment, it still doesn't make sense to him. But he responds by asking where else they would go. Simon Peter is saying we have seen too much to go back now. We might not understand this, but we believe in you, and we're not backing down. We've lived under an open heaven and will not go back.

It's a profound statement, and I find myself resonating with Simon Peter's response so much. When I read these sentences, I think back to times in my life where Jesus has asked me to do something, and it makes no sense to me. I don't understand it, but I just know that I trust Him.

Just like Simon Peter, I have asked, "Where else shall I go?" I will not go back so it looks like we're stepping forward, hand in hand together, whatever that looks like.

I want to encourage you right now that Jesus is so much better than what we can think or imagine. He has given every single one of us who believe in Him the ability to live underneath an open heaven because that's what He purchased with His blood for us. And I'm going to save you some trouble and let you know that most things He asks you to do aren't going to make sense at first. It will require a constant leaning in to His presence and voice, but man oh man, is it so worth it.

It's where faith and logic crash, and we get to choose which one we want to submit our lives to...

ANOTHER IN THE FIRE

("Refiner": Maverick City)

MY SECOND YEAR OF MINISTRY SCHOOL WAS JUST AROUND THE corner, and I was returning to California after the most painful summer of my life, while also one of the most beautiful. Weird tension, I know. There were a lot of family things that unfolded, and my world was flipped upside down that summer. I was relieved to get away and be in the space I knew would make me feel safe to process and grieve. But nothing in me could've known that it wasn't just a painful summer, but that I was about to go through a very painful year as well.

Now let me start off by saying that I have had really painful seasons before where Jesus felt really distant to me, and those seasons just felt so deep, dark, and lifeless. The difference with this season was while feeling a lot of pain, Jesus was the nearest He had ever been to me, and my relationship with Him was the strongest it had ever been. I had fully given Him my life this time, so there were still a lot of days filled with joy and laughter too.

I find it funny how we think it's either or. Either you're sad or you're happy. You're lonely or content when, in actuality, I learned that it was both and (sad and joyful, lonely and content).

It was the beginning of my second year in ministry school that Jesus showed me I had suppressed emotions for so long. It wasn't that I couldn't feel things; it was that I wouldn't allow myself to. For so long, when I was addicted to pornography, I would constantly feel numb. I lived in this state of feeling numb for long periods of time and learning how to function out of that place. Have you ever felt like you were living in survival mode? Not truly living but functioning from a place just to get by? That was where I found myself having this realization that I was using my addiction as a means to survive, though I really wasn't thriving at all.

It became clear to me that silence was my biggest fear. It might sound silly, but the thought of being by myself in solitude gave me so much fear, and I couldn't figure out why. For years, I actually believed that I was an extrovert because I was always doing things, around people, and constantly remaining busy in some way. But the more I started on a journey of healing in my life, I quickly realized I had put that label on myself because being alone actually terrified me, and I would do anything possible to remain busy and distracted. I am actually a very social introvert, but my lack of healing made me put a label on myself out of fear and upholding a reputation that I thought I had to be someone I wasn't. I wonder what labels you have incorrectly placed on yourself out of a place of upholding a specific reputation. What distractions do you have in place, keeping you from becoming all that you are created to be?

That year, 2018, was a really personal year for the Lord and me. There were many days and nights I spent alone in my room and car, as I felt His kindness ushering me to open up to Him and let Him come into my heart. You see, I realized I didn't trust Him with my past, my hurt, and my pain. I couldn't see where He was in all of that struggle, so I avoided addressing it, and in turn, avoided bringing the most vulnerable parts of me to the Lord and our relationship. There were also a lot of parts about myself that I didn't love, and when you spend time alone with yourself and your thoughts, those parts come to the surface.

You can only run from yourself for so long. I was running from who I was rather than embracing who He made me to be.

I realized that I had separated my past from my present. The problem was that I was seeing them as two separate people, when in order to actually love the current Allecia, I also needed to love past Allecia: all her flaws, mistakes, and pain.

In order for you to love the present you, you need to choose to forgive and love the past you, all the mistakes, hurt, and pain along the way. If Jesus loved you at your worst and deemed you as someone He wanted to spend eternity with, we can no longer look at ourselves as unlovable.

It can be easier to love who we are after we have come to Christ sometimes, and we tend to look at our lives as being two separate things, when really it's all intertwined. Jesus doesn't look at us as "before Christ, after Him." He is as in love with us before and after we are saved. He is rooting for us and championing us all the way through, fighting for us during every stage of our lives. So why would I choose to love only the part of me I thought was good enough and not realize that I've been enough the whole way through?

That year, I made the conscious decision to let Jesus into all the parts of my life I had stuffed down for so long. The pain that I had avoided, the hurt that I had felt. I walked through deep pain from a romantic relationship I was in that year where God asked me to lay it down. I walked through mindsets and patterns that I had believed about myself that needed some serious realigning. I walked through immense trauma where He kindly and lovingly walked me through some of the deepest pain I had ever known and experienced, which had been stuffed down inside myself since I was little.

It was by far the scariest thing I have ever done because my fear in being alone was that I would come to the conclusion Jesus wasn't as good as I thought He was. I don't know why this was my fear, other than I was having a hard time trusting Him with my emotions and my heart. To me, it was the scariest thing to think I could bare my soul and trust that Jesus would come in and heal, only to find out He wasn't as good as I thought He was.

And do you know what? I found out that Jesus wasn't as good as I previously thought. He was way better than that and kinder.

There was one time specifically where He was walking me through some deep inner healing. He took me back into a vision I had seen countless times with Him before in order to walk me through some trauma that happened when I was younger. I had come a long way and received a lot of healing, but I still didn't trust Jesus as my protector. This was a really hard realization for me to accept, because it wasn't a quick-fix solution. I knew that the Bible said He is my protector, but my experiences weren't lining up with that truth.

I was mad, and I was hurt.

I could've easily put on a nice façade, acting like everything was okay and praying a nice prayer asking God to show up as my protector and call it a day. But I was so over putting on a front, especially to the One who I had just spent all year opening up to. So, I let Him have it.

I can remember driving in my car at night just days before He walked me back through the vision, with tears streaming down my face. I had prayed a nice, little prayer just seconds earlier, and then I lost it and my true emotions started bubbling to the surface. "I don't trust you to protect me. I don't trust you to keep me safe. I'M MAD. I'M SO *BLEEPING* MAD. I'm sitting here in pain, and I feel alone and I'm tired of being nice about it. I'm so hurt and angry." That was followed by one of the loudest screams I had ever heard in my life, coming from my own mouth that felt like it started deep in the bottom of my stomach. It was as if years of pain were coming to the surface, and I was just now letting myself feel the gravity of it.

That's probably not the nice, little prayer you would've thought I would say, and, to some of you, that might even seem down-right rude. But if there's one thing I learned through that year, it was that Jesus wasn't scared of any part of me. He wasn't scared of my emotions, my pain, and my anger. I had suppressed anger for so long because it didn't seem right, but I felt I was given full permission to express it to Him. Now, I understand that He is the Holy One, the righteous One, but might I suggest that if He didn't turn away from Saul killing Christians, or Judas betraying Him, He probably wouldn't be turned away from a few choice words yelled out in anger from a place of trauma either.

And wouldn't you know that after choosing to be real with Him and with myself, healing entered in. He took me back through that vision He had countless times before, but this time, I could see Him in the room. This time, I could see the angels who were present when trauma was occurring. This time, I heard His voice loud and clear say, "Allecia, I wage war on your behalf."

Those words were the sweetest balm to my tender open wounds, and I crumbled all over again before Him, seeing Him as my protector for the first time in my life. Those words have stuck with me every day since, and He has continued to show me since then where He was and how He was already working out everything for my good and for His glory. In the thick of pain, I could see how all these years later, He had been orchestrating a plan for redemption and healing. How He was making me spiritually aware of Him moving in every area and stage of my life, which drastically changed my perspective on pain and who He is.

Let me just say this. There are some of you who need to just get mad. There are some of you who need to cry. There are some of you who have feelings so bottled up that need to be let out. He is not scared of your emotions and your pain. He knows all of it anyway and, like a good and loving Father, is waiting for you to come in close and crumble before His feet.

Let me remind you that Jesus, Himself, was not exempt from pain. He allowed Himself to feel it. The following verses tell us more on this truth.

Matthew 26:38: "My soul is overwhelmed with sorrow to the point of death."

John 11:35: "Jesus wept."

Luke 19:41: "As he approached Jerusalem and saw the city, he wept over it."

Isaiah 53:3 (NLT) says, "He was despised and rejected- a man of sorrows, acquainted with *deepest grief.* We turned our backs on him and looked the other way. He was despised and we did not care."

And He reminds us where He is in the middle of all that pain. Psalm 34:18: "The Lord is close to the brokenhearted and saves those who are crushed in Spirit."

If He is near in our pain, then we can come fully honest about what we feel, laying it all out before Him. But the healing doesn't come from just revealing the pain. We must make a conscious decision to let Him into those areas of our hearts, revealing His truth to us and bring His healing touch that ultimately transforms our lives.

You see, He was always there for me. He was always waging war on my behalf. But my experiences had clouded that and formed lies contradicting His Word. But in His kindness, God spoke truth all over again to my tired, weary soul. It wasn't easy, but it was the most freeing moment.

When we let ourselves become exposed fully before Him, God does what only He can do. Listen, I'm all for therapy, counseling, etc., because that can be super helpful and has been extremely beneficial in my own life, but only the person of Jesus will truly change you. Only the person of Jesus will transform you with the guidance of the Holy Spirit. Only the person of Jesus can set you free.

To let yourself be refined is a wild concept. During that second year of ministry school, I felt like I had willingly placed myself into a furnace. Of course not literally, but figuratively and spiritually, I had said, "Ok Jesus, you can have whatever you desire."

The song mentioned above in the beginning of the chapter talks about wanting to be purified by letting the Lord have whatever He desires. That is a wildly dangerous prayer to pray because He will answer that prayer in a radical way. But it will require letting go of the way you are used to doing things, and being real before your God. It will require confronting all the parts you've put in so much work to avoid addressing. It comes from a place of deep surrender, truly letting Him have His way fully in your heart.

In His kindness, Jesus'll call you into the fire when you're ready. I wasn't ready my first year of ministry school, as He needed to build trust between us first. He needed to break down some walls and set the groundwork for what He was going to do the following year. Because when He comes and refines a person like only He can do, He comes with an everlasting renewal, giving you life abundantly with truth and hope that goes down deep. He refines with the intention of longevity in mind and is in it for the long haul with you.

A.W. Tozer put it this way in his book, *The Knowledge of the Holy,* "A right conception of God is to worship what the foundation is to the temple; where it is inadequate or out of plumb, the whole structure must sooner or later collapse" (1961). He rebuilds the structures and knocks down the unsteady bases so that when He rebuilds, we will have an everlasting structure built on a firm foundation that will not crack because it is rooted in the truth of who He is and who He says we are.

I want to share a part of a journal entry I had written from that year when I was right in the middle of some really deep pain, when He was rebuilding my foundation.

January 1st 2019:

I need to see you as an eternal Father. An eternal Father who loves His kids eternally. There was never a temporary thought in your mind when we were created. You love long-term. I feel so messy and broken right now but God, I'm asking you to step into my pain with me. I can't do this without you. I'm strong but it's because I'm getting my inner strength from you. Jesus, this is the hardest thing I've ever been through. I pray that when the pain is so great and I can't take it anymore, and I'm feeling that deep emptiness, that your love would be even greater. Your love would be even louder. Giving me strength to face the pain when I need to and filling me up with deep love when I can't look at it any longer. I'm going to choose to trust you. I will choose you, Jesus, even if that means laying my heart and pain down in surrender over and over again.

I've tried to go back to sleep and Jesus, my heart is literally in so much pain. Please come fill me up. I need you, and I don't know how to do this without you. I desperately need you.

Re-reading that entry even now gives me so much hope. That above paragraph sounds really raw, and it definitely felt so permanent when I wrote it. Most nights that year, that was the cry of my heart. My simplest prayer became an utterance of the word "help" and barely getting out the words to say, "I need you." But I look back on that year and see how much fruit was produced from that time of growth. How much freedom was found. That the scariest fear of God not being enough had been faced head-on and proven false.

He is near to the brokenhearted and longs to walk in your pain with you, bringing you out the other side victorious. I promise He's so much closer than we know. And He longs to show you how near He actually is.

"I will not leave you as orphans; I will come to you." (John 14:18)

"The thief comes only to steal and kill and destroy; I have come that they may have life, and have it to the full." (John 10:10)

There is purpose in the pain, not that He caused it but He's too good to not turn it into something beautiful. He can't help but bring beauty from ashes, for He is after all the Redeemer of life.

Isaiah 53:5: "But he was pierced for our rebellion, crushed for our sins. He was beaten so we could be whole. He was whipped so we could be healed." (NLT)

This verse is ultimately talking about sin, but it leaves me in awe reading about the wholeness the Lord brings. When we think of what He did on the cross for us, we understand He paid for our sins, but it also covered everything that sin entails. Someone else's sin and the effect it had on you, hung up on that tree. Bondage to anxiety and depression, abuse and trauma, pain and loss, sin and mistakes hung up on that old rugged cross. The thing you find yourself in right now, the brokenness you feel, was paid for. He was beaten so that He could make you whole. He was whipped so that you can be healed: spiritually, physically, emotionally, mentally. We tend to look at that word "whole" and apply it to our sin, that our sin was bought with His blood. And that is 1000% true. But His blood paid for you to be whole in every way. The blood paid for the ramifications and effects of sin. Your healing was paid for in the blood; your restoration was paid for in the blood; your emotional well-being was paid for in the blood; your thought life was paid for in the blood; your whole story was covered by the blood of Jesus.

His pursuit for you was poured out in red as He was whipped and beaten, pierced, to make you whole. His body broken and crushed to make yours whole again. His relentless love keeping Him on a cross to bring you freedom.

LOVE HAS THE FINAL SAY

("Lost In Your Love": Brandon Lake, Sarah Reeves)

IN MARCH OF 2019, A CAR ROLLED UP TO MY APARTMENT AT 3:30 a.m. to take me to the airport. I walked down my steps with my suitcase in hand, looking up at the sky as the rain poured down hard. I had waited in anticipation the night before for this trip and barely gotten two hours of sleep. My team and leaders from Bethel were all meeting at the airport to head on our mission trip to Brazil.

We had been meeting as a team for months, praying, planning, and dreaming of all that would take place in Brazil. It seemed surreal to all officially be at the airport together preparing to make the journey to this beautiful country. After forty-two hours of traveling, we finally landed in Recife, Brazil.

I was so excited! I remembered everything that Jesus did the year prior in Mexico, and I couldn't wait for everything that He would do this year in Brazil. I was more confident, more prepared, and was so excited to step out and just go for it, watching Him work through me. Man, did I not know a thing that was coming, though.

It seemed like every opportunity where there could've been the ability for me to do something of any significance, it was given to someone else. Every time we led a prophetic session, or someone shared something, I was always asked to serve or to help out in really practical ways. I was so confused because I didn't feel trusted as a leader, by my group or by God. I started questioning if I was capable of leading at all, if anyone thought I had anything of value to bring. Most importantly, I was so confused with Jesus. You see, that year He had been showing me that my voice had been shut down for years. He had taken me back to moments in my childhood where I would find a microphone (literally and figuratively) and start speaking. From a young age, I would practice these motivational speeches or sermons, and as I grew up, I knew that was a calling on my life.

Little by little, though, that little girl became terrified to use her voice, due to fear and personal life experiences. Fear overcame me, and anxiety would consume me anytime I went to speak. The Lord had started working on that area in my life during a preaching class I was in that year, and I had assumed the Brazil trip was just going to continue to help with that even more. Instead, I felt defeated that no one was picking me to do anything special.

I asked myself some really hard questions during the first few days of the trip. Everything felt like it was being stripped back, and I questioned that if I didn't do a thing for Jesus for the rest of my life, if I never amounted to anything, if I never saw another healing or miracle, if another prayer wasn't answered, would He be enough for me? Was His love enough for me? At the end of the day, all of this is really just about love. Is that enough?

Those were painful questions to ask, because I was scared of the answers. Do you ever have those questions that you're genuinely scared to ask because you're afraid the answer you are terrified of hearing will be true? That's exactly what I was going through, and it wasn't helping that I had another layer of questions paired with those.

Right before the mission trip, what I didn't tell you was that I had messed up. It had been a while since I had fallen into old patterns and sin, but I caved in one night when I was feeling pretty numb and frustrated. I had been doing so well and didn't understand what caused me to backslide. I had gone through years of renewing my mind, which was such a process since it had been extremely distorted. And I was doing well overall, so I couldn't understand for the life of me why this addiction seemed to be back knocking on my door.

One night, we were about to lead a service, and our team was given some alone time before we had to meet to get ready. I was feeling so defeated with what I had done and with not feeling qualified at all to be on this trip when the Lord spoke to me. I asked Him what He wanted me to do that night. He said, "You will receive breakthrough when you come to me like a child."

Ok, I thought. *Great, well, I already feel helpless right now so I guess we'll see what you do with that.* We arrived at the service that we would be running, and I was asked to call out some words for physical pain in the crowd that I felt the Lord saying, and then pray over those people for healing. *Finally,* I thought, *God is going to use my voice after all.*

The night was going to start with worship, and then from there go into our team-sharing things and preaching. Worship started, and we were about ten minutes in when my eyes started to water with tears. I could tell that I was really going to start crying so I sat down on the ground. Normally, I'm not concerned anymore with being that girl with tears running down her face during worship and can care less if people see me like that. But this was different. I just wanted to not be seen in that moment, so I put my head in my hands as I was sitting on the concrete.

All of a sudden, I broke down uncontrollably sobbing. I'm talking that ugly crying, shoulders shaking, snot-dripping kind of crying. Like, it was not cute. Not in the slightest bit. The trauma that I had been working through all year was culminating into this moment. I had this massive realization that everything I had struggled with, in terms of sexual sin, was tied to trauma when I was younger, and fear had consumed my life ever since then. My face was planted on the floor at this point, and I realized that my crying was the loudest thing in the room. Not exactly the subtle vibe I was going for.

I couldn't stop crying, and it became clear that my cries were louder than the worship. I was absolutely that girl in the back on the ground louder than anyone in the room having an encounter with God, and I always swore I would never be her. I remember thinking, *I'm the one that's supposed to be serving these people and speaking and leading, and I'm on the ground an absolute mess. What kind of a leader is that?* I was given money to go on this trip to serve others, and I can't even do that right now. I was supposed to be here to love on God's kids, and I'm the one on the ground having an encounter with the Lord.

And then came the sweet words of Jesus, "Are you also not worthy of my pursuit? I said I leave the ninety-nine to come after the one, and you are the one."

"Yea, Jesus, but I can't be doing this right now. I'm supposed to be leading," I said.

It was at that exact moment that my leader from the trip got down on the ground and kneeled next to me. "Whatever is happening, Allecia, whatever the Lord is doing in you, let Him do it. You don't need to get up; you don't need to do anything. You can stay right here all night."

Wow. That was so freeing. It was as soon as those words were spoken that I felt shame break off and was given a vision from God.

Jesus first told me that He's not just up there in heaven wiping away all my sin, but He actually gets down in the dirt with me and lovingly takes the rough soil out with me. That He lovingly sifts through the parts that are causing harm in my life and transforms it into good soil, where good things can grow forth. Where true transformation can happen. Then I saw myself standing in front of Jesus with a dress that looked like rags. He told me it was time to hand it over to Him, that I was wearing a dress that was never mine to wear. He gave me a new dress, the most beautiful dress that I had ever seen. It was stunning and was glowing white. "This is the dress that I purchased for you. You no longer will put that other one back on," he said.

All of a sudden, His love came crashing over me. I understood He was talking about my purity. He released me from trauma and fear and brought in freedom. That whole year, He had been showing me about the holiness of Jesus. He was redefining holiness in my life personally, and there was a new standard being defined. Even things that weren't necessarily bad just didn't fit my mold anymore for what I could do. There was a fresh conviction coming over me of how I was to be treated, what I would tolerate, and what I would fight for. It wasn't prude; it was purity in its purest form.

I wanted Him to show me how to speak and how to step out and do things, but He just wanted to show me His love. It's funny really. The thing I thought I wanted wasn't met, but the thing I actually needed, and the question I had asked, of whether His love was really all worth it in the end was answered. He always knows exactly what we need.

Second Timothy 1:9: "He has saved us and called us to a holy life-not because of anything we have done but because of his own purpose and grace. This grace was given us in Christ Jesus before the beginning of time."

I fully believe I was set free at that time from thinking I was broken due to my sexual sin. That didn't mean I didn't still struggle after, for it would still be quite the process to walk out that freedom. The difference was I knew that I was free, and it wasn't a part of my identity. The Lord spoke true identity over me and reminded me of who I was and how He saw me, giving me a clean slate all over again. It was, however, something I had been consumed by for so long that I had to learn how to walk that out with the Lord. A lot of it was realizing triggers and learning how to now operate from a place of freedom when facing them. When all you've known for so long is captivity, it can feel very normal to go back to that, so you have to choose to lean into the new normal, which is your freedom He paid for!

I believe that there are some of you who need a fresh viewpoint of things.

A fresh viewpoint of your freedom, your purity, your circumstance, your promises He's spoken over your life. Take a moment and ask Him to give you fresh eyes to see what He sees.

His perspective changes everything: redefines, remolds, and realigns. It brings your perspective back into focus and is abundantly more than you even knew you needed.

His perspective allows you to see the pursuit He's had over you this entire time, planning a story better than anything you could have ever imagined.

PARADISE

("Homecoming": Bethel Music, Cory Asbury and Gable Price)

IN BRAZIL, THERE WERE MOMENTS THAT LEFT LASTING IMPACTS ON me for the sheer reality of what my eyes had witnessed. One night, our team separated into smaller groups and partnered with an organization in the area who provided resources to girls selling themselves on the streets. It's incredibly shocking to see sex trafficking and prostitution right before your very eyes and is not something you can ever unsee. I can distinctly remember watching men packed into a car drive by slowly or wait on the street corners for the girls to stop talking to us so that they could get in the car. It's hard to forget the conversation you have with a young woman who starts crying, telling you she doesn't want to do this any longer. It's also infuriating to have a conversation with young teen girls selling themselves on the street corner, while a man in his fifties sits on the side, eating a cheeseburger and getting pissed off that we are taking so much time with them. It's gut-wrenching to learn these girls are fourteen and sixteen, one is currently pregnant with her second child, and when I ask how they know each other, they exclaim they are sisters. Their mother only knew the streets as a means to get by, so she sent them out from an early age.

My heart was grieved with compassion for these sweet sisters, and one of the girls on my team asked if they had ever encountered the Holy Spirit. They said they knew who God was but didn't know about the Holy Spirit. The woman on my team placed her hands over one of the sisters' hands, but never actually touched the girl's hands physically. The sister exclaimed, "I feel heat, I feel fire!" She started laughing and shaking her hand, exclaiming, "It won't leave; it's still here." She was moved by the fact that God encounters people like that and has physical interactions with them. We, as a team, were moved by the fact that God would encounter her physically and give her a new memory when it came to physical touch, one that I believe was healing and comforting.

There was another day we had the privilege to go to a safe house, a place where young girls resided in after being rescued from sex trafficking. We watched a young girl, about the age of twelve, who had been trafficked ever since she was little, receive the Holy Spirit and be absolutely blown away when she started speaking in tongues. She had no idea what that was, had never heard of it, but ran around the house in pure joy and shock at what was happening. This carried on for quite some time, and once it finally subsided, she told us in Portuguese that it wouldn't stop, and she couldn't make it stop even if she had tried. I asked her later to pray over me, and with tears streaming down her face, she prayed. I have never in all my life felt the presence of God moving through a young girl in the same way I did through this sweet girl.

Why do I share all of that with you?

Because it's not just my personal story of God's pursuit over my life. He will reach His children no matter where they are. He will find them in the trash dumps of Mexico, in a college dorm room, in the church, in a rehab center, on the streets of Brazil as they sell themselves for the fifth time that day for money, and in safe houses where they were rescued. I saw a personal God on this trip, a God that saw His kids hurting and in pain and needing to know He saw them and cared about them personally.

I saw a God inviting them to have a relationship with Him. I saw a God who came to them. Culture so often thinks that we need to go to God first; we need to find Him, and in every other religion, that is the case. Christianity is the only religion where my God meets me. He finds us in the mess; He finds us in the sin; He finds us in the pain and steps into it with us. He is not afraid of the darkest places that you've found yourself in. He will find you in the thick of it.

But what about when you feel worthless, not good enough or too messed up and broken? One of my favorite moments of the whole trip was when our team went to conduct an outside church meeting where anyone in the community could come. We spent time talking to the Brazilians there and just connecting with them. And then I saw him. I saw this man who looked like the life had been sucked out of him, like life had taken everything from him, and he was left with nothing. Instantly, my heart felt the love Jesus had for this man, and a group of us decided to go over to him.

Moments prior, we had seen him sniffing glue and getting really high.

We walked over with our translator, and I felt this boldness come over me, prompting me to ask him if he wanted something better than the drugs he was currently doing, to which he hesitated a little and then answered yes. It felt like I was operating in an authority other than my own, since I would not normally be that direct, but it was clear that Jesus really wanted to meet with this man.

My team and I started to share with this man about Jesus. I was in the process of sharing the story of Jesus on the cross and how He died for the sins of the world that anyone who believes in Him would have eternal life.

"One of the criminals who hung there hurled insults at him: 'Aren't you the Messiah? Save yourself and us!' But the other criminal rebuked him. 'Don't you fear God,'; he said, 'since you are under the same sentence? We are punished justly, for we are getting what our deeds deserve. But this man has done nothing wrong.' Then he said, 'Jesus, remember me when you come into your kingdom'" (Luke 23:39-42).

This was when the Brazilian man interrupted me and said, "I'm too messed up though. You don't know what I've done. God can't forgive me, and He didn't forgive that man on the cross either." He looked deeply saddened when he said these words.

That's when it hit me. This man had never heard the second part of the story. I asked him, "Do you know how the story ends though?" He looked up confused and responded no.

Luke 23:43: "Jesus answered him, 'Truly I tell you, today you will be with me in paradise.'"

It didn't matter what the man had done. He himself knew that he deserved the death he was facing because he committed a crime worthy of punishment and death. But he also knew no one could save him apart from the Son of God. He recognized the Savior of the world next to him, and Jesus assured him that he was forgiven, that he would be with Him forever in paradise.

I looked at the Brazilian man sitting in front of me and realized he was no different from that man on the cross. He had done a lot of horrible things in his life, but he was desperately needing a savior. And Jesus was meeting with him right in that moment, just like he did with the man hanging next to Him on the cross, letting him know he was forgiven and set free.

I shared with the man that he could wait until the very last second of his life to surrender to Jesus, just like the man on the cross did, but Jesus wanted to give him freedom, joy, and love right now.

I will never ever forget the intensity in which the man looked at me when I talked, taking these words in that he had never heard before. Truth will do that. It will break all the boxes you've placed Jesus, and yourself, in. And I will never ever forget the tears in his eyes as he listened. The love of Jesus will soften the hardest of hearts and will break off years of shame in a person in an instant.

We prayed with him, and as we were walking away to leave for the night, my heart was still so consumed with the love Jesus had for this man that I turned away and walked right back up to him. I looked at him straight in the face and said, "Jesus loves you so much." I just kept saying it, and I watched this man's eyes brim up with tears. I asked if I could hug him, to which he said yes, and I embraced him.

I will never forget the look on that man's face as he encountered the love of Jesus for the first time, as he heard truth for the first time, heard he was forgiven and set free. Also, I will never forget the feeling of love I felt for this random stranger in Rio de Janeiro, Brazil, who I had never met, and the way in which Jesus broke my heart for this man that He loved.

Isn't that just like our Jesus though? To go to extreme measures to love His kids. To set them free and bring them hope and love. That night, that man received hope for the first time. He was told he was loved beyond measure.

A man who had done more bad things in his life than I probably wanted to know, doing drugs to cope with the loss of everything in his life, was moved to tears in front of his friends because Jesus met with him through an American girl on the streets of Brazil. The love of Jesus sees a person in a crowd, and His eyes are fixated on them; that will never stop blowing me away.

It takes me back to the parable of the prodigal son all over again.

Luke 15:20:24: "But while he was still a long way off, his father saw him and was filled with compassion for him; he ran to his son, threw his arms around him and kissed him. The son said to him, 'Father, I have sinned against heaven and against you. I am no longer worthy to be called your son.' "But the Father said to his servants, 'Quick! Bring the best robe and put it on him. Put a ring on his finger and sandals on his feet. Bring the fattened calf and kill it. Let's have a feast and celebrate. For this son of mine was dead and is alive again; for he was lost and is found.' So, they began to celebrate."

It's just like the Father to welcome you in with open arms, to have you trade in your old rags for riches. To crown you with royalty and celebrate your return to Him, no matter what you've done. He cares way more about you choosing to be with Him than what you've done.

You don't enter the kingdom with shame; you get to enter in with celebration because the price has already been paid for you.

Brazil,

You were the place I received true freedom. You were the place my heart was poured out before the Lord. As I sat in the houses of your people, ministered in your streets where women lined the strip to sell themselves, and prayed with the men getting high because they didn't know hope existed, I faced a reality that was bigger than my heart could handle. I laid out on the floor of your country, recognizing my utter dependency on the Father. Brazil, I went to show you that the Father is pursuing you relentlessly. But I walked away feeling the pursuit of the Father over me in a fierce way that I didn't know I needed to see. He is so kind, and I will never forget what He did in my heart in Brazil. Eternally grateful.

So today, I encourage you to think about this question. Are we really living a life that was worth someone dying for? Are we still in chains and sin when all of that was dealt with at the cross? Are we fighting for things that have already been won for us? Victory is our inheritance, and freedom is our anthem. You see, it was Jesus's love that put Him on that cross. No nails would've been able to hold down the King of Glory if He wanted off. And our sin wasn't strong enough to keep the Messiah there. But He chose to go for your sake to bring eternal life and freedom; he would bear the weight of sin and defeat death to be with you forever. Your value and worth isn't a light matter; you are costly and worth someone dying for. You were once seated in prisons of your own story, but His blood paid the price for you to sit in new places. His love is relentless for you.

Out Of The Ashes

("Before and After": Elevation Worship, Amanda Cook, Maverick City)

HAVE YOU EVER HAD A DREAM IN YOUR HEART FOR SO LONG THAT BY the time it finally comes to pass, you have to pinch yourself that it's actually happening?

That's how I felt when I found out my family was going to Italy for a vacation. Being Italian, it was a dream I had in my heart since I was a little girl to go. I always knew I was going to go one day, but it felt surreal when it came time to actually go.

We packed up our bags and headed to Europe where we would spend the next three weeks. I specifically remember praying before we went that I would be able to have fun and enjoy the trip, that I would be able to just be me and be present. Those kinds of prayers were normal for me before going somewhere or doing something, and I didn't really think much of it.

We all had the best time, and I had so much fun the whole time we were there!

And then we came back home, and I started working at the summer camp I had worked at for the past few summers as a counselor. About three weeks in, I had this cloud that just came over me, and it became really dark. This cloud wasn't new; I had lived my life going in and out of it, but this time, it felt really dark and numbing. It started to freak me out because I felt lifeless, and nothing was helping relieve it. Anxiety crept its way in briefly, which also freaked me out because it was something I had battled heavily with the year prior. I quickly gave that anxiety to Jesus, like I had learned to do the whole year prior, and it left. But the cloud still remained. The word "depression" bounced back and forth in my mind, but as quickly as it would enter, I would just as quickly send it away.

You know those days when you're sad, and it takes everything in you to fake it so that you can do your job and be present in what you're doing? Yea, I had had those days before, but nothing within me could make myself fake it on this particular day. I was lifeless in front of the kids I was leading, and I knew I couldn't stay. I went home early that day, knowing that I needed to figure this out. I couldn't possibly be battling with depression. I'm not a depressed person. I don't have suicidal thoughts, and never have. I've never self-harmed. I just need some time alone to figure out what's wrong, and then I'll be fine, I reasoned.

Earlier that year, I was sitting in a class during ministry school when one of the pastors was talking about how what you are born into affects you more than you think. He was giving the example of someone being born into deep depression and sadness, where that child was quite literally born into depression and operated more from that place than they knew because of the environment they were born into. I sat there thinking that I was possibly born into that environment but pushed it aside, reasoning that I wasn't.

So here I was, sitting in my bed, after coming home early from a workday, and staring at the wall in front of me dazed. I didn't want to confront the question and couldn't handle the possibility that I maybe had battled with depression for years.

Ever since I could remember, it was really hard for me to enjoy having fun, hard for me to be present. There were moments where I could be fine, and then hours later, I would go blank, as if my light, airy mood just felt sucked out of me. It felt as if I was living in and out of a cloud constantly. No one ever knew it because I became really good at faking it when I was in the cloud. Of course, it was only fake on the outside. Internally, not confronting the sadness and ignoring it would make me feel even more sad and disconnected. Even going to bed wasn't something I looked forward to because there were so many mornings I would wake up with this deep sadness consuming me. I didn't have a reason to be sad, but I just would be. Until you go through something like that, the feeling is extremely hard to explain. You learn to not confront pain and function out of survival mode; despite the deep sadness you have. You don't understand why you feel like that, and think that something must be wrong with you, but you don't even know how to begin to describe that to someone, so you stay quiet.

It wasn't until I started to confront pain and hurt in my life the year prior that all of this started to surface. I realized how it wasn't normal to be living like this constantly. It sounds funny that it wasn't abnormal to me prior to that, but I just thought it was the way I was because it had been that way for as long as I could remember. As soon as I started healing from the pain, I saw that living in the absence of confronting pain was doing more harm to my joy than I knew possible.

I'll never forget that day, after coming home early from work, sitting in my bed and letting myself come to the realization that I had suffered with depression for years. It shook me to my core because I didn't want that to be a part of my story. I didn't want to be another girl who had overcome something else. I didn't want to have to work through anything else and was tired of the process, tired of growth. I was just exhausted, and the thought of this newfound realization was too much to bear.

Deep in my heart, I started to accept that what I was so terrified of admitting was true. That word, depression, scared me because the thought of that label was overwhelming. And as I began to let tears flow down my face, something completely unexpected happened.

That word that seemed so scary, that I had secretly been questioning for months, brought so much clarity. But rather than it labeling me, it allowed me to have a clear vision to see that it wasn't me but was this thing that I'd been struggling with for years. As soon as I chose to acknowledge it, I was able to separate the word from my identity. There was such a fear of that word defining me, but instead, a peace came over me that it was a struggle, not an identity. I thought that acknowledging it meant acknowledging that I was a depressed person. But I instantly recognized I was a person dealing with depression, not a depressed person. I'm a firm believer in only speaking life over yourself, and depression is not my identity.

Everything started to become so clear. For years, I had thought something was wrong with me because I had taken depression on as my identity. But now, I have clarity.

Shortly after sharing with my mom about depression, she shared with me that she had wondered if I had battled with it. She was on her way to work one day shortly after finding out from me I was dealing with that when she started having a conversation with the Lord. He showed her that I was born into deep depression and sadness. The circumstances in which I was born into were not life-giving. My mom herself was going through depression because of everything going on in her life, and I was brought into that.

Now, I never shared with her about the sermon I had heard months prior and that I had wondered if I had been born into something similar. But that night, when she came home from work and we had dinner, she shared with me all that the Lord had spoken to her that day. I couldn't believe the Lord had showed her this very thing I had only heard of through a pastor months prior and never shared with anyone. She apologized to me and prayed for me that the spirit of depression I was born into would be broken over my life. I felt something physically lift off me and instantly felt lighter.

I had been going on a journey of feeling emotions, self-aware-ness, love and acceptance from the Lord for the past two years, and this realization propelled me into the depths of break-through I'd never known. Sure, I still get sad and yes, I now know how to feel pain deeply and in a healthy way without staying in that place, but that day, I was completely set free from depression and have never faced it since.

And this is where I interrupt the story.

The above paragraph was written about two years ago, and at that point in my life, I truly hadn't felt depression again. Today, in 2024, I have a different story to share.

I could easily gloss over this part of my story and leave it at what I had written two years ago, but I want to be transparent and show that the journey with Jesus is not always linear.

There can be a stigma sometimes in Christianity, especially Charismatic movements, where once you have been freed from something, or delivered, that is it. You don't deal with it again. And because of that, I didn't want to admit that I was struggling again, two years later, deeply with depression. It felt invalidating to what God had done previously, as if it wasn't solidified and didn't fully work.

It made me question the blood of Jesus and what He paid for and what I thought I was freed from. It made me question what was wrong with me. You see, I had gotten to this place where I shut off emotions again, enabling me not to connect with pain at all, leaving a numbing that was all too familiar, and depression slowly crept its way back in, until it flung upon the door completely and started wrecking havoc in my life. I knew the patterns all too well, the numbness toward feelings, both negative and positive, the moments of silence you fill with distraction, the loss of purpose and hope felt, and the isolation you seclude yourself in. The scrolling on your phone to avoid going to sleep, because you will be alone with your thoughts. But at the same time, the relief of letting your head hit the pillow to shut off the numbness that you feel.

Depression and I have had our battles, to say the least. And if you have struggled with depression at all, I want to say that I get it. I understand. It's hard to explain to someone who has never felt the weight of it. It's hard to make sense of it when everything in your life is going good, and you feel it creeping back in. And it's hard to make sense of what freedom looks like when you're facing a battle you thought was already won.

But I want to remind you that the battle HAS already been won!

As much as I'm all for self-care and awareness, I'm completely aware that freedom this deep can only come from Jesus. "Now the Lord is the Spirit, and where the Spirit of the Lord is, there is freedom" (2 Corinthians 3:17).

And I want to remind you that if you are struggling with depression, that is not your identity. That is not who you are. You are not a depressed person; you are a person dealing with depression. And I want to encourage you that you will come out of it. Maybe you are someone who, like me, had been set free of depression, and lately you have felt it creeping back in. To you, I want to encourage you that the blood of Jesus is still enough. The enemy wants you to stay stuck in isolation and your own thoughts, feeling guilt and shame creep in that you are somehow back at the same place, dealing with the same thing yet again. But God wants to meet you in it. And I would encourage you to ask God to fight this battle with you.

For me, when I was facing anxiety and depression, I made a list of verses in the Bible to combat anxiety (with peace) and depression (with joy), and then I wrote down the solutions to those things I was struggling with. For example, if I was feeling anxious, I would pull up my list I made and see the verse in 2 Timothy 1:7 that reminds me that I have a spirit of power, love, and self-discipline. I would speak that over myself and then ask God to remind me that that is the reality I live from. I would look for another solution and see that in 1 Peter 5:7, we are told to cast our anxieties on the Lord. So, I would tell Him what I was anxious about. And then leave it there with Him. I would start my morning like this and do this all throughout the day. And wouldn't you know that I slowly started experiencing more peace than anxiety, more joy than depression.

The simplest things overwhelmed me again with pure joy and gratitude: the crisp morning of a fall day, a kind person paying for my coffee, the summer night heat you feel on your face as you drive around at night with the windows down. Everything was vibrant again. Jesus's voice was in everything, and I could find Him in anything and everything.

All during ministry school, people would constantly tell me that I carried so much joy and that God was going to really use that in my life. I used to get so annoyed by those statements because I kept thinking, *That's not me; I don't know why you're saying that.*

Someone once said to me, "Your joy is lethal to depression." It made absolutely no sense to me then, but afterward, I saw how even two years prior when that word was spoken to me, the Lord knew He would set me free from what I didn't even know I was imprisoned by. That once again, I would look back and get to see He was in the details the whole time.

And joy, I realized, isn't based on my ability to feel good or be happy, thank God. That true joy can be in the middle of your deepest pain. Wanna know something funny? I had some of the deepest joy I had ever felt in the middle of the hardest year of my life. There were days I would catch myself with the biggest smile on my face because the deep peace and joy I felt made absolutely no sense for the circumstance I was in. I learned that it's not one or the other. That you don't need to have figured out all your stuff and then feel joy. That's called happiness, and happiness is a fleeting feeling. But joy, true joy, can be found and felt in the deepest of pain. Only true joy can enable you to go from crying tears of sorrow to tears of gratefulness twenty minutes later because you felt the nearness of your God in the middle of your pain.

Hebrews 12:2: "For the joy set before him he endured the cross, scorning its shame, and sat down at the right hand of the throne of God."

This verse blows me away every time and gave me so much hope when I came upon it again in such a hard season. When I was reading it a year ago, I was so moved by what I was reading that I decided to write something for me:

For the joy that was set before Him
a rugged cross stood tall
the smell of blood encircling still
the raw, cracked hands and drying blood from His pierced hands
and feet
there laid my Savior, a crown on His head
yet in His agony, He could be heard uttering the words,
"Father, forgive them for they know not what they do."

Father, take this cup from me, He had cried out hours before
But if not, your will be done.
He endured.
He endured for the joy set before Him.
Joy is the pressing in for the greater ahead.
The reality of living in the present while knowing what's to come.
Gazing into the Father's eyes full of hope and expectancy,
Knowing He is good and true to His word.
Your kingdom come,
Your will be done,
On earth as it is in heaven.
The joy that surpasses happiness because joy was never a feeling, but a choice.
If He chose joy in the midst of surrender,
We get to choose it too.
He paid for joy in all circumstances.
His suffering was not in vain.
Enter in through the gates of joy and praise,
The anthem of heaven,
The victory dance of the generations of the King.

I want to encourage you with this writing. Jesus felt emotion very deeply and also never let emotions rule and dictate His life. He never pushed aside His feelings and deemed them as "not important," but He also never let them have the final say.

My hope is that this chapter encourages you to come to Jesus with all your feelings, all your emotions. To know that choosing to feel, while it could be scary, brings you healing and freedom, and ultimately brings you closer to God.

To know that you are loved right where you're at. But where you're at isn't where you're going. That the story isn't finished, and that hope always has the final word. He will never belittle your feelings, but He will also show you that they don't define you. That your feelings are not your identity.

And when you have no faith for the days ahead? Well, then you're in the perfect place because He's the one that gives faith.

Ephesians 2:8-9: "For it is by grace you have been saved, through faith-and this is not from yourselves, it is the gift of God- not by works, so that no one could boast."

Romans 10:17: "Consequently, faith comes from hearing the message, and the message is heard through the word about Christ."

And when you have no joy for the days ahead?

Psalm 16:11: "You make known to me the path of life; you will fill me with joy in your presence, with eternal pleasures at your right hand."

He gives faith for the days ahead, and He gives fullness of joy in His presence. Thank God none of this is dependent on us! Our only job is to come to Him; He does the rest.

So let Him come and fill you today with fresh perspective, fresh faith, and fresh joy!

For the joy that is set before you…….

COOKIES AND MILK

("Goodness of God": Bethel Music)

IT WAS THE DAY BEFORE HALLOWEEN 2019, AND I WAS THE ONLY one home in my apartment. I had a long, eventful day and had just finished cooking dinner for myself. The house felt so cozy, and I propped myself up on a kitchen stool and placed my dinner in front of me. I was looking forward to having a chill night and turned on an episode of *Friends* to watch while eating dinner. There's just something about a home-cooked meal and a favorite show that makes for the perfect way to end the night. About ten minutes into my meal, I heard a knock on the door. There wasn't anyone that was supposed to be coming over, and my roommates weren't home so it surely couldn't be for them. Shrugging my shoulders, I assumed if it was important, they would knock again. Then came another two knocks. Reluctantly, I got off my chair, figuring I should answer. I was excited to have a night of quiet and relaxation, and really was not in the mood for any interruptions. Didn't they know I was watching my favorite episode for what must've been the tenth time?

I opened my front door to see three young women my age standing on my front step smiling. *Oh*, I thought, *they must have the wrong house.* "Hi," they exclaimed, "we live in another apartment in this complex, and we were just praying and asked God what apartment we should go to, to bless someone. He told us apartment 74, so here we are at your apartment."

Caught off guard, because it's not everyday people show up at your house because God sent them, I welcomed them into my house. They proceeded to hand me a bag of chocolate chip cookies that were hot off the oven and a mason jar full of milk.

I'm pretty sure my mouth dropped open at this point. What they didn't know at all was only two days prior, I had told one of my roommates how much I wished there was a delivery service for cookies and milk because I was craving them so much. Now, I not only had my favorite cookies but was literally hand-delivered them the exact way I had wishfully wanted them only two days prior. I'm not normally someone who wants a whole glass of milk with my cookies, let alone ever wanting just milk to drink, but for some reason, I was really craving it earlier that week. When they handed me the jar of milk, it was in a mason jar, which is my absolute favorite cup to drink anything in, and the only cups I would drink out of at home.

They then proceeded to hand me cash, telling me that they felt they were supposed to give it to me for coffee. Anyone who knows me knows that 90% of the time when you see me, I am going to be holding a coffee. It might not be in the typical list of love languages, but it's for sure my love language!

The girls went on to hand me scriptures they had written down for me and prayed over me, praying all these things that I had been talking to the Lord about that no one else knew.

It's impossible to walk away from something like that and not feel deeply loved; I felt so seen and known by Jesus.

As much as I love when He shows up in the big ways in my life, it hits my heart differently every time He shows up in the small details. In the cries of my heart that only He knows. In the details that matter to no one else, but they matter to Him.

Earlier that week, I told God I just needed Him to be a dad to me. I thought I needed His words, but He showed me that I really had just needed Him to hold me and to show me practically what love looks like rather than just using words. He comes in ways we don't always think of, going to ridiculous measures to show us He cares, but that's what extravagant love does.

When we open the door to His invitation, even maybe reluctantly at first, He will always enter in joyfully.

Sometimes I think about what would have happened if I didn't open the door. I mean, it was my house after all; I didn't have to open the door. I could've sat there, enjoying the rest of my night in peace, watching my show and eating dinner. But instead, I forgot all about my dinner after they left. I went to my room and just cried (shocker, I know), spending time just worshipping Jesus. His love had crashed in on me that night, and I felt such gratefulness. I then watched a movie later that night, eating my cookies and milk. When my roommates came home, I was so excited to share with them what had happened. The goodness of

God will do that. It runs hard after you, and when you have a head-on collision with it, you can't help but bubble over with joy and tell others.

I wonder how many doors He's knocking on tonight. How many encounters He has just waiting for people that are willing to open the door. How many people He wants to show up for in a different way than what we are asking for or expecting.

His love chased me down that night. His love knocked on my door and told me I was seen, loved, and deeply known. His love is chasing you down. Will you open the door to let Him in? Will you walk toward it, or will you ignore the knock because it's an inconvenience?

Jesus knocks a lot more on our lives than we give Him credit for. We are usually just too busy to hear the knock or open the door.

Come expectant this week to be interrupted by the goodness of God chasing you down, and be ready to hear Him speaking to you.

First Chronicles 16:34: "Give thanks to the Lord, for He is good; his love endures forever."

PURSUIT

("Graves Into Gardens": Elevation Worship, Brandon Lake)

IT WAS A SUNNY MORNING, AND MY TEAM AND I FROM MINISTRY school were about to make the two-and-a-half-hour drive to Sacramento State, which we did monthly to share Jesus with students walking around campus. There, we had watched multiple people get healed, set free, and give their lives to Jesus. This day in particular, I decided to write an encouraging word on a piece of paper. In short, this letter was telling the person I would encounter how much Jesus loved them. I love doing this and blessing someone in this way, but this time I decided to ask the Lord for a name for who He wanted me to give this letter to. I heard the name "Camila" (not the actual name). Normally, I would just keep that knowledge to myself and would see if I came across someone with that name. But this day in particular, I felt an urging to write the name on the front of the letter. I folded the letter up and put it in my back pocket. All day, we talked to people, but I never met anyone with the name Camila.

We were nearing the end of our time on the campus, but our team decided to gather together first to worship outside with a guitar before leaving. A professor came over and started weeping as he stood there with us and then had people pray over him. Another student asked for prayer and said she felt so encouraged seeing Christians who loved Jesus like this because she hadn't seen it in a while. Another man gave his life to Jesus while we were there.

As I sat there, taking it all in, I started to walk along the exterior of where we all were worshipping. I asked the Lord who He wanted me to go talk to. Immediately, I noticed this girl sitting off to the side on a ledge with a grey beanie. I knew instantly that I was supposed to go talk to her. I started making my way to her, and another girl from my team joined me, saying she felt God also leading her to go talk to this girl.

We introduced ourselves to her when we approached her, and she told us her name was Nicole (also not her real name). We asked her if there was anything she needed prayer for and told her that if there was, we would love to pray with her. She hesitated for a second before saying yes. Nicole then explained to us that she normally wouldn't say yes, but that it had been a really hard couple of days for her. Her sister had just unexpectedly passed away earlier that week, she told us. After giving our condolences, I then proceeded to ask her what her sister's name was.

"Camila," she answered.

Instantly, my eyes filled up with tears as I started to understand the holy moment God was orchestrating. Reaching into my back pocket, I pulled out the letter. I explained to her that earlier that day, I had written a letter for someone, and God had given me a name to put on the front of it. I had been looking all day for Camila. I then handed Nicole the letter and said that God had her sister in mind, that He knew Nicole needed peace about how Jesus felt about her sister. That He deeply loved her late sister Camila.

I will never forget Nicole's face as she took the letter in complete shock and, with tears in her eyes, exclaimed that she never cries. She kept saying, "I can't believe God talks like this." Nicole was someone who had been in church before, but she was encountering the tangible love of Jesus in a way she hadn't before. We spent the next two hours with her, praying, talking, laughing, and just spending time together.

Unfortunately, because of COVID-19 starting to spread at that time, we were not able to go back to that campus after that day. I messaged Nicole one day, letting her know that we hadn't forgotten about her (we said we would get together with her next time we were there) and wasn't honestly even sure if she remembered me. Her response told me she hadn't, as she explained that she keeps the letter in her car with her.

It moved me to tears all over again. The God of the Universe knew that day that Nicole would be sitting on that ledge. He knew I'd ask Him for a name, and He was more than ready to give me her sister's name. It dawned on me later that He could've given me Nicole's name, but He gave me her sister's. Why? Because He speaks into the details of our lives, making them personal. When I spoke her sister's name, something that had so much pain behind it, it let Nicole know there was no way I would've known that, and all of a sudden, it became very personal. Jesus became real, tangible. Because He stepped into her pain. He called her out personally and spoke to her heart directly. And the message was clear, "I see you."

Jesus, in His kindness, would give this girl something so personal from His heart that she would keep it in her car as a reminder. Because He relentlessly pursues His children.

The more I get to know Him, I see how extreme Jesus's love is. The more I let Him exchange my idea of love for His, I see the insane measures He takes just to love on His children. He's so personal, so intentional.

That day, Jesus had Nicole in mind when we arrived on that campus. And it made me think, *How much more would we see God move if we just stepped out?* Like simply writing that letter, or those girls simply asking the Lord who they should bless by coming to my door.

If we actually believed that our obedience changes history, what amazing things would happen. God can move however way He pleases, but He wants to move through obedient sons and daughters.

His love was never meant to be bottled up inside of you; it was always made to overflow. Your expression of love was always made to be a reflection of His.

At this point, I hope you believe that Jesus wants to use you to advance His kingdom. That you will see so many beautiful things in this life by simply listening to Him and stepping out in obedience.

And I hope you believe Jesus is so in love with His people, whether they know Him or not. That He longs to be with every single person and will go to deep measures to show them.

If you don't believe in either of those things, that's ok. His character isn't dependent on if you agree or disagree. He will love you and pursue you the same regardless. But I'd encourage you to ask Him for a way in which you can step out to see His kingdom advance this week. And I'd encourage you to ask Him to show you that He's pursuing you.

Every step He takes toward you is an invitation to let Him capture your heart...

RELENTLESS LOVE

*("Nothing Else": Cody Carnes; "Move Your Heart": Upper Room;
"Alabaster Heart": Kalley)*

"YOU FEEL A SENSE OF BELONGING IN THE PRESENCE, AND THAT'S what tugged you here. The more of Him." This sentence was spoken by one of the female leaders, Leslie, at Bethel and solidified exactly what I had been searching for, for years. The more of Jesus. The more of Christianity. His presence.

Inside each of us is a desire to feel like we belong. Whether we want to admit it or not, we all want to be a part of something, something bigger than ourselves. We all want to feel known, seen, and valued. We all want to feel like we matter.

When asked about ministry school, I am usually asked what impacted me the most during my time there. While many individual stories and moments come to mind, I consistently find myself trying to describe the worship that changed my life. And every time I struggle to find the words to adequately come close to describing something that can only be experienced.

How do you describe a room full of hundreds of people worshipping into the wee hours of the morning because they just love Jesus? How do you come close to explaining the praises that would turn into shouting and dancing at three am, because the Lion of Judah was in the room? The stillness of peace as His presence filled a place. The knees that bowed to the ground because the weight of holiness that entered the room was too much to stand any longer. The unity felt because everyone's attention was on Jesus. The freedom to express yourself however you wanted in worship. The roar that would erupt as what started off as singing that every other god is an idol, turned into a holy declaration as the reality of what we were saying became tangibly felt.

It's hard to describe the holy moments where all you can do is weep under His presence. And it's harder to describe the war cries that come from within as you sing and declare resurrection life over a little girl in your community. When you've fought for things in the Spirit with people beside you, it creates a deep, permanent bond. A bond that says these are your people, through and through. When you've sung, prayed, and declared heaven into being when no one else said it made sense. When there was a group of people wild enough to believe what Jesus said and to worship from a place of victory and hope, that is worship that will mark you. That is worship that will never leave you the same.

Worship isn't a feeling, a check to cross off for good Christian duties, or even a setlist. It's not coming from a need to perform a religious duty, but rather is a posture of your heart. It's a life-style, a total abandonment of self to amplify and exalt the One who is worthy. True worship is undignified and unrestrained. Worship, in its purest form, is the emptying of self to be filled with the fullness of Jesus. And that's not just through a song, a dance, or a prayer. Those are the expressions that come from living in a lifestyle of worship. A permanent vertical posture where your attention is solely fixed on the One who reigns in heaven.

Bill Johnson, senior leader of Bethel Church, says this phrase, "When I see His face, I wish I'd given more away." I want to see His face this side of heaven and just continue the friendship we've already built this side of eternity when I arrive at heaven's gates.

So, who is Jesus to me?

Jesus is the invitation-bringer. He gives you a glimpse of who He is and simply asks if you'd like to see more. He never leaves me out, never picks me last or keeps me on the sidelines waiting. He never cancels me because I don't understand or think differently than Him. He's not afraid to get into the mess with me and help me sort it out. Not because He wants to fix me, but because He loves me. He is never ashamed to be seen with me and isn't scared of the questions I bring to Him. He's not easily put off by my emotions and lovingly corrects me when I'm wrong. He never condemns, but always convicts. He is the man with holy fire in His eyes, burning forever with a love so deep for me that I'll only scratch the surface. He's held me in the darkest of night and celebrated me on the brightest of days. He's my freedom fighter, the One who declares my victory is already won. He's my source of strength when I have none. He's my confidence, reminding me of who I truly am. He's a life of adventure and endless surprises. He's my promise keeper, telling me to dream bigger and then cheering me on all the way across the finish line. He's my reminder of what's possible, for He's the God of the impossible made possible. He's the One that trusts me enough to carry His heart. To trust me with His people and His nations. He has stood in the coldest of rooms, waging war on my behalf, and held my hand through every triumphant victory. He's never one to rush me past my pain but slows me down to find Him in the middle of it. He's not just a part of me. He's my lifeline, my source, my constant need, and my every desire.

He's my Healer. Provider. Comforter. My justice. My peace. My joy.

He's the One that saw me on the cross saying I never want to live without her. He's my listener, my confidante, my quiet whisper, and the loudest of roars. He's the kindest and most humble, the most powerful and mighty. The most patient and forgiving. My refiner and redeemer.

He found me when I was lost and celebrated me when I came home. He's my most faithful friend, and He's fiercely loyal to the end.

He's the One who refused to keep "till death do us part" in the vows and tore the veil for all eternity so not even death would keep us apart. He wreaked havoc in hell to bring me back the keys. He's the One who trades my tainted stained dress and calls me holy and blameless.

Jesus is the most holy, radical person who ever walked this earth. He defied every religious rule and shook the crumbling foundations of this earth. I haven't given my life to a religion, a set of rules, or a God who sits on the throne, unbothered by the things of this world. I have laid my life down to a King, who tears down the strongholds of religion and pride, who delivers the nations from freedom, who commands the angel armies to move on my behalf. I serve an active God who very much cares about every detail of my life.

What they didn't tell me in church growing up was that following Jesus requires laying down your own agenda. That it would cost me more than I ever thought; that's just the reality of it. But they also didn't tell me that it's impossible to count a cost when what you receive in return is priceless.

I don't have all the answers, but I know that I've seen too much to ever go back. I had to be refined by Him, to know how deep my beliefs went. I had to come to this knowing deep in my bones that when everything is stripped away from me, I will choose Jesus, time and time again. What He gives me in return is beautiful, but He is the One I'm after. Not what He can do for me, but who He is. He is worth every single yes. No matter what way you cut me, I will bleed Jesus. It's always been about Him and always will be.

In short, He's my pursuer.

He relentlessly loves me. Relentlessly fights for me. Relentlessly pursues me.

His relentless love has won my soul.

THE INVITATION

("You are Loved": Maverick City Music)

Fallen idols, erected from these hands you created,
Built with hearts of pain and pride, desire and greed.
Oh, how you've showed us your freedom,
But we traded a heavenly lullaby for the hissing of snakes.
These towers they soared,
Our chests swelling with triumph,
But you scattered our work like the Tower of Babel.
We laid at the altar of sin and grief,
Forgetting the altar of repentance and grace.
How ever will we pick up the pieces of this debris?
Our hands are cracked, our hearts bruised.
We need the potter to put back the clay.
You say throw into the fire every evil desire
And make room for the new canvas, to tell of your glory.
Disruption and chaos abound,
But can't you see we're standing on holy ground?

The Lion of Judah has come to rebuild.
The potter is here, now melt in like the clay,
Letting Him form and remold,
Till every idol is crushed
And every knee bowed.
The desire of the nations,
Come be our only desire.

I FEEL JESUS DOING SOMETHING HOLY IN THIS HOUR IN HISTORY. He's restoring the hearts of His people back to Him. He's shaking our foundations so that anything not of Him will crumble. He is rebuilding and refining.

He is unifying His church and preparing His bride (the church). Like the spoken word I wrote above, I feel like our idols have lied to us for too long. Now, you might hear the word "idol", and think, *Well I don't follow Buddha, or Allah, or any other god except God.* But let me remind you that if Jesus is not the main thing your life is centered around, you have an idol in front of him. An idol is anything you give the ultimate priority to in your life, and it determines how you live your life. And your idol doesn't even have to be a bad thing. It can be a career, your relationship, your weightlifting body you work so hard for. None of these are bad things, but when they take priority over Jesus, they become an idol. Maybe for you, you idolize the idea of marriage, sex, alcohol, people-pleasing, your image. Or maybe, you would say, you have tried other ways to discover spirituality, whether that is through another religion, crystals, tarot cards, etc.

Whatever it is, culture has tried to sell us the lie that pursuing earthly things (materialistic), fleeting emotions (happiness), and other means of spirituality (alternative sources to find purpose) is the main goal. But I'm here to tell you that anything placed in front of God is a distraction to your relationship with Him. Two things cannot be number one in your life. Trust me, I've tried. I placed my reputation, my image, my pornography addiction first before God, letting those control and dictate my life. I let my anxiety, depression, and pain have the final say in my life, ultimately idolizing trauma and making it bigger than what God says about me and the story He's writing with me. Culture sells us this idea that we can do it on our own. We can figure out our purpose, heal ourselves, find a higher power that works for our lives, but I am telling you, true freedom is and can only be found in Christ. You are the freest you'll ever be when you are the most dependent on God.

I'm going to share a dream with you that I had a few years back.

In the dream, I could see a stage that looked something like the Red Rock Amphitheatre in Arizona. Behind the stage was a massive mountain. On the stage, there was a bunch of people leading a worship set. And as they worshipped, I saw fire start to come down the mountain. The fire started to cascade down, fiercely making its way toward the stage. As it began to hit the stage, it completely enveloped the worshippers. It's important to note that this fire wasn't physically hurting anyone; it was just engulfing them. I was in awe as I watched these worshippers continue to worship, being unfazed by the fire. I could see another group of people who had been in the crowd, and they had started to run as soon as they saw the fire. As they ran, they turned back to gaze at the stage and were deciding if they should stay or continue to run. Before they had time to decide, the fire consumed them as well. And then there was a third group of people who as soon as they saw the fire coming, took off running, not ever looking back. And the fire consumed them as well.

I woke up from this dream knowing that it was a prophetic dream, and a few months later, the Lord revealed to me the meaning of the dream.

He showed me that the three groups of people were representing three different walks with the Lord. It's also important to note that the fire here was referring to the refining process of the Lord, burning up anything in their lives that weren't of the Lord, and the baptism of the Holy Spirit, leaving people with boldness and power.

The first group, the worshippers on the stage, were representing people who would say they are sold out for Jesus. They have given their whole lives to follow Him and have centered their lives around Him. If this is you, you probably have gotten to a place where you have learned to not put God in a box. That you want Him to come however He wants to, but you ultimately don't care what it looks like, as long as He comes. Your gaze is fixed on Him, and He said the worshippers who truly worship me in Spirit and truth will see my Spirit poured out (John 4:24). But I also felt like the Lord was wanting to remind this group of people not to ever get used to His presence. I'm going to assume if you would say this is you that you probably have had your fair share of encounters with God and have history with God. But you cannot live on the encounter from three years ago. We cannot get used to the presence of God. We can't take it for granted when He comes, and we feel His tangible presence.

It can be so easy to make these things normal or brush them off the longer we are on our faith journeys. But I feel like the Lord wants to give you a fresh fire and hunger that you had when you first got saved, mixed with the maturity of your faith now. The solid foundation you have built with the Lord, with the hunger returning that you once had. The awe you once carried. The fire in your belly when you would hear a testimony about the goodness of God, or He answered a prayer, or you saw a miracle for the first time. He is pursuing you with a fresh fire to carry you into this next season. He is convicting and refining you of things that might feel uncomfortable at first, but they are to bring you into greater freedom. He is coming with a fresh baptism of His fire to equip you with boldness and power, to prepare the way for Him. He is pursuing you with a desire again to hunger and thirst for Him. He is restoring in you this fresh hunger to burn for revival, for Him.

Then there was the second group of people. You might find yourself in this group if you have a relationship with Jesus or are on the fence about following Him. You might be like me when I was in college, one foot in and one foot out. Not sure if you really want to fully commit to this life. You might be seeking answers or are approaching the Holy Spirit with hesitancy. You might have a lot of knowledge about God, but less consistent experiences with the Holy Spirit specifically. If this is you, I feel the Lord is going to come and encounter you with a love that you've never known before. Some of your questions will get met just by an encounter with His presence, and for others, you will start going on the journey with Him as you ask Him the questions you've been scared to ask. There are some of you who would find yourself in this group, where maybe you have done the "good" Christian things for a long time, grew up in the church, and follow God, but you have never had an encounter with God. I am telling you knowledge is good. Knowing the Bible is good. Praying is good. But you need an encounter with God, you need to experience the tangible presence of God. Even right now, take some time and ask God to encounter you. Don't be surprised if He answers right away, or days later when you are doing something random, like making dinner. He loves that prayer; He loves a hungry heart; and He loves to meet that request.

And then there's a third group, the ones who ran away immediately. To you, the Lord isn't scared that you're running. By now, I hope you realize how loved you are. God cares about every detail of your life (Psalm 37:23). How He is always pursuing you. His reminder to you is that you are not left out of the family. You, also, are the family He left heaven to get. There has been a pursuit over your life, and even though you might have found yourself running, He is running harder after you. How do I know that? The fact that you are reading this book is an indicator that God wants you to know Him more. Not because of anything I've said in here, but by the way in which God has been speaking to your heart and revealing things to you, bringing freedom and healing to you. You also are in need of an encounter with the living God, and He wants to meet you by revealing more of Himself to you.

For our God is a consuming fire (Hebrews 12:29).

There's an invitation into the fire in this hour. To once again, or for the first time, let Him shake up anything in you not of Him. To let Him redefine who He is to you. Not what religion or other people or even the church said He is. To truly give Him your whole life to see Him for who He truly is. To ask yourself what you want your story to be, what legacy you'll leave behind, and what is really worth living for. What do you want to have mattered at the end of your life? Is it enough to say you lived a good life, had the nice house, nice friends, the good paying job? Or does your heart burn for something more? To have unshakable joy, a hope in your future and eternity, and a plan for your life that far exceeds anything you could've ever done in your own strength? Do you long to have greater freedom and healing, living from a place of peace and confidence that only God can give?

My prayer for you is that through this journey we've gone on together in this book that you saw the faithful hand of Jesus weaved throughout my story, and the stories of others I've shared. I pray that you felt an invitation to enter the adventure with Him, no matter where you are at in your journey.

He has extended an invitation to let Him relentlessly pursue you; that's who He is. Your yes or no won't dictate His choice to pursue you, because He can't help but pursue, but your yes back will open your eyes to the reality that He is and has been pursuing you. The reality of that pursuit will radically change the course of your life. There is so much more He has for your life, friend.

He's a pursuer through and through.

His pursuit for you is relentless, and always has been.

So, I leave you with this: the first question is for you to answer, and the second will be answered by Him.

Who is Jesus to you?

Who are you to Him?

Matthew 18:12: "What do you think? If a man owns a hundred sheep, and one of them wanders away, will he not leave the ninety-nine on the hills and go to look for the one that wandered off?"

His relentless love will always go after the one.

Who Is Jesus To You?

_____

_____

_____

_____

_____

_____

_____

_____

_____

_____

_____

Who Is Jesus To You?

Who Are You To Jesus?

_____

_____

_____

_____

_____

_____

_____

_____

_____

_____

_____

References

page 40: Barna Group, "The Porn Phenomenon," *Barna*, accessed on April 27, 2024, https://www.barna.com/the-porn-phenomenon/#:~:text=Teenage%20girls%20and%20young%20women,12%25%20among%20older%20men).

page 40: Covenant Eyes, "Pornography Statistics," *CovenantEyes*, accessed on April 27, 2024, https://www.covenanteyes.com/pornstats/

page 40: Webroot, "Internet Pornography by the Numbers; A Significant Threat to Society," *Webroot by Opentext*, accessed on April 27, 2024, https://www.webroot.com/us/en/resources/tips-articles/internet-pornography-by-the-numbers

page 48: Kris Vallotton and Bill Johnson, *Supernatural Ways of Royalty: Discovering Your Rights and Privileges of Being a Son or Daughter of God*, 2017

page 112: A.W. Tozer, *The Knowledge of the Holy*, 1961

Printed in the USA
CPSIA information can be obtained
at www.ICGtesting.com
JSHW011455140724
66391JS00001B/1